Praise for
Dating Never Works . . . Until It Does

"*Dating Never Works . . . Until It Does* is more like sitting down in a Jacuzzi with a close friend talking about relationships and mistakes and love and deep hurt than reading something your mom bought for you because she's worried about your chronically single state. It's candid, it's real, it's funny, and it reminds you that sometimes you just need to change a few small things to see the results you've always desired."

—Taylor Church
Author of *I'm Trying Here: A Memoir of Love, Loss, and Misadventure*
and *Return Not Desired*

"Zack Oates is a force to be reckoned with. When observed in the real world, he seems larger than life and unhindered by any degree of skepticism, pessimism, or criticism. But when you read his book, it's clear that below the intrepid exterior is an individual who has spent a lot of time looking for meaning, understanding, and companionship. In *Dating Never Works . . . Until It Does*, Zack condenses his lessons laboriously recorded over his years of extensive dating into pithy aphorisms and candid anecdotes. As somebody who is unabashedly unafraid to live life to its fullest, Zack challenges the reader to go out into the world and see what life has to offer, by taking chances and learning to see the opportunities around them. Prepare to think. Prepare to laugh. Prepare to snort while you laugh. Prepare to look around the subway in embarrassment because you snorted in public. And finally, prepare to reroute yourself onto a different train once you realize you've missed your stop because you were so engrossed in this book. It may not happen exactly like that, but prepare for something similar."

—Stephen Nelson
Documentary filmmaker

"Zack speaks to us with a level of sincerity and realism that allows us to not only see his human imperfections, but also find our own. Through his stories and experiences, we see ourselves and how we might improve. This isn't a book exclusively for those looking for love. This is a book for anyone who wants to better understand love. Oh, and by the way, he's outlined his points with genuinely entertaining stories and comedic encounters. One of the thrills of dating is the newness of it all; the novelty of fleeting passion and sudden whimsical notions

of romance. The thrill of this book is Zack's gentle presentation that, perhaps, love can re-emerge each day. Maybe, just maybe, we can see each new day as a chance to win the love and affection of our partners, either in dating or marriage. That is why I must recommend this book for people both inside and outside the populated realm of "the singles." Anyone who enjoys a light-hearted read with deeply rooted meaning can find purpose and personal application in *Dating Never Works . . . Until It Does*. The result will likely be a more satisfying understanding of love, and subsequently, more fulfilling relationships."

—Cameron Gade
Award-Winning director and writer, entrepreneur, overall baller

"Zack is a dear friend with a genuinely good heart . . . and that's where this book comes from. I love his perspective and would recommend this book to anyone who is single . . . or even just looking to improve their relationship. He is able to take the frustrations of dating and give actionable advice woven with hilarious stories. Read this book!"

—Scott Jarvie
Entrepreneur, professional photographer, author, and traveler

"This book is a must-read for anyone who wants a lasting, loving relationship. Even though I have been married for twelve years, I deeply appreciate the advice on how to strengthen current relationships. Invest your time in this book and it will pay off in one of the most, if not the most, important areas of your life—your significant relationship."

—Jessie Funk
Youth advocate, bullying prevention expert, motivational speaker
Author of six books, including *The Lost Art of Ladyhood*

"Dating as an adult is hard and unpredictable. It's like looking both ways before you cross the street and getting hit by an airplane. In the era of Tinder and eHarmony, it's nice to have someone like Zack Oates to guide you [through] the steps that come after 'swiping right.'"

—Creighton Baird
Producer and YouTube star with DevinSuperTramp
Entrepreneur and adventurer

"Reading the book is like reliving history. I lived it every post-date, with the phone call about the first date, the excitement, the falling in like and sometimes loveish, the frustration, the pain, the recovery, . . . and then the sense of hope, and cycling back to the excitement of the next first date. Zack shows how creativity and hope, along with emotional fortitude, gives great hope to those is the dating world. One thousand first dates have led him to a beautiful, amazing wife that is the perfect fit for his genuinely unique personality."

—Michelle Oates
Entrepreneur, philanthropist, and Zack's mom

"I wish I had this book when I was single. Zack is able to use his 1,000+ dates to help others to navigate the dating field from both the emotional and practical side. It is a great read. Recommend!"

—Steve Young
Hall of Fame quarterback, married at 38

"Zack has given us a rare look into the world of dating from a male perspective. Written in a very casual conversational format, this book is as entertaining as it is insightful. Zack has the ability to mix religion, humor, and candid honesty as he reveals what going on 1,000 dates has taught him. I found this book to contain practical advice and perceptive insights for anyone interested in exploring the mechanics of developing lasting relationships."

—Kristeen L. Black
PhD, Specialist in religion and family studies,
Author of *A Sociology of Mormon Kinship: The Place of Family Within the Church of Jesus Christ of Latter-day Saints*

"This book is a great combination of personal experience, wit, and practical wisdom (did I mention wit?). Zack has an uncommon perspective offered to anyone who finds dating to be a challenge and would like to have a better experience. Read it, enjoy it, apply it, live it, love it."

—Klayne Rassmussen
PhD, marriage and family therapist, author of *The FrogBuster: A Girl's Guide for Survival in the Dating Swamp* and *Beyond the Spell for Teens: What Guys and Girls Wonder about Each Other*

"Mr. Oates has the rare gift of being able to speak about (let's be honest) a difficult subject with humor, experience, and most of all sincerity. You know that crazy aunt of yours who keeps bugging you about being single? Zack is the exact opposite of that. Zack treats the reader like a true friend. He cares about you and understands your frustrations and genuinely wants you to find happiness. Though he has a lot of steps, how to's and suggestions, you never get the feeling of arrogance or back-patting, just a guy who went on way too many flipping dates, learned a lot, and compiled those into an immensely enjoyable book. For those of you who have already found your eternal adventure buddy like I have, the "Give Up Now—You Will Never Stay Married to the

Same Person" [section] alone is worth the investment. This book is literally for everyone, even that crazy aunt of yours."

—Jason "The quiet introvert dentist turned comedian how the heck did that happen" Gray, YouTube celebrity, Studio C

"This book is written in a very down to earth style. Zack treats dating as an event to enjoy and not stress over. After reading this book, a person should sit back, take a sigh of relief, and realize that finding that right 'someone' happens when dating is treated as a journey and not as just a 'project' to . . . get through. Remember to be yourself!"

—Susan and Trent Whittle
Married 50 years

"This book contains a comprehensive guide to finding the forever love of your life. If you follow the advice in this book, you won't waste a lot of time and energy on a lot of pointless first dates and just keep dating and dating and dating like our "professional dater" grandson did."

—Nani & Reid Ivins,
Married over 60 years, Zack's grandparents

"The principles in this book will lay a foundation for a happy marriage that will last as long as ours. Zack's insights gained validity and strength with . . . years of dating and looking and hoping. Like he says, giving service and love to each other is key to long-term marriages."

—Onalee and Steve Wood
Happily married for 50 years

DATING NEVER WORKS

...Until It Does

100 LESSONS FROM 1,000 DATES

ZACK OATES

Plain Sight Publishing
An imprint of Cedar Fort, Inc.
Springville, Utah

ISBN 13: 978-1-4621-1927-1

Published by Plain Sight Publishing, an imprint of Cedar Fort, Inc.,
2373 W. 700 S., Springville, UT 84663
Distributed by Cedar Fort, Inc., www.cedarfort.com

LIBRARY OF CONGRESS CATALOGING-IN-PUBLICATION DATA

Names: Oates, Zack, 1986- author.
Title: Dating never works ... until it does / Zack Oates.
Description: Springville, Utah : Plain Sight Publishing, An imprint of Cedar
  Fort, Inc., [2016] | Includes bibliographical references and index.
Identifiers: LCCN 2016038593 (print) | LCCN 2016041857 (ebook) | ISBN
  9781462119271 (perfect bound : alk. paper) | ISBN 9781462127078 (epub,
  pdf, mobi)
Subjects: LCSH: Dating (Social customs)--Religious aspects--Church of Jesus
  Christ of Latter-day Saints.
Classification: LCC HQ801 .O23 2016 (print) | LCC HQ801 (ebook) | DDC
  646.7/7--dc23
LC record available at https://lccn.loc.gov/2016038593

Cover design by Kinsey Beckett
Cover design © 2016 by Cedar Fort, Inc.
Edited and typeset by Deborah Spencer

Printed in the United States of America

10 9 8 7 6 5 4 3 2 1

Printed on acid-free paper

Dedicated to my one-in-a-million girl. I count it a blessing that it only took me 1,000 dates to find you.

CONTENTS

Contents

Contents

Contents

FOREWORD

I was single and living in India working at a leprosy colony when my perspective on dating, marriage, and life really solidified. In my adolescent mind I thought that marriage was the end of the road—the end of fun, adventures, and freedom. People were always telling me, "You better get it out of your system now before you get married." To be totally open, I was in Asia hiding from dating and marriage and I felt a little guilty for it. I mean, wasn't I supposed to want to find someone to complete me?

It was at this time I first heard the story of *The Missing Piece Meets the Big O* by Shel Silverstein. It is about an unhappy wedge-shaped character called the missing piece who is searching for another shape with a void of its exact proportions to fit into. "The missing piece sat alone . . . waiting for someone to come along and take it somewhere." After trying many different unsuccessful fits with depressing results, it finally meets the Big O who has the ability to roll on its own. The Big O rejects the missing piece, but it helps the piece realize that it doesn't need someone else, the piece just needs to start moving. The missing piece starts to flip over and over until it eventually wears down its edges, becomes a circle, and begins to roll by itself! At the end of the story the Big O and the missing piece end up together because they realize they are each other's perfect fit—not because one couldn't go without the other, but because they wanted to roll together.

The woman who shared this story with me was a successful businesswoman in her late thirties who had never been married. In talking to me about dating she said, "I'm not looking for someone to complete me; I'm looking for someone that can roll with me."

That's when I decided I was going to make my life awesome, no matter if or when I got married. That's when I decided I was going to be happy and not look for someone to complete me. And that's when I decided I was never going to stress about dating, or feel guilty for it.

I had never heard of Zack or his dating blog before we met (even though we had over 100 mutual friends). When we started going on dates, one of the first things people would ask me was, "You know he's dated like everyone, right?" Honestly, if I had known about the cereal dating (pun intended), I probably wouldn't have gone out with him. I'm not the alpha female type who likes to compete for the biggest prey. Looking back now, I'm so grateful I started the relationship with those blinders. I see now how all of his dating experiences have made him a wonderful person and make him appreciate me more. (And can I just take a second to thank those 1,000 other dates for not marrying the best husband in the world? Seriously!)

And as for my fear of marriage? Moving to a new city, visiting ten countries, going on dozens of weekend trips, and starting a business—all in our first year of marriage—proved to me what it means to roll together.

This is a wonderfully written book, and I loved reading it! It made me laugh and it made me cry. The hilarious stories and inspiring lessons encourage you to be your best and have fun along the way, no matter what life has in store. Look, even if he wasn't peering over my shoulder right now as I'm typing this, I'd still tell you to give this book a shot. Trust me, your life will be better for it, regardless of your relationship status.

Remember, dating is fun, so don't stress. And it's only you who can make the decision to have an awesome and complete life—so start rolling.

—Annie Oates
Traveler, entrepreneur, and wife of the guy who wrote this book.

INTRO

DATING NEVER WORKS . . . UNTIL IT DOES

S o, there are a lot of reasons why you might be reading this book.

Maybe someone bought you this book and you're not sure if you should be offended.

Maybe you are in a bookstore wondering if you should keep reading.

Maybe you just are looking for some ways to enjoy dating more.

Maybe you found it at a yard sale, or saw it posted online, or misunderstood the title, or just went through a breakup, or just met someone special . . .

Whatever your reason, hi.

I'm genuinely glad you're here.

And regardless of the reason you're reading this, I think it only fair to share with you the reason I wrote it.

See, it took me over 1,000 dates to find my wife. I learned a lot of lessons along the way (from personal experiences and friends) and documented them over the course of ten years. Some of those lessons have withstood the test of time, and this book is the compilation of the top 100 lessons.

All the stories you are about to read are real (and by the end you'll probably be shocked I ever was able to get married). We will go through being single, getting dates, what to do on those dates, how to build up to a relationship, dealing with breakups, overcoming discouragement, and eventually, love. Look, things are going to get real up in these pages. We'll talk about God (though not religion), laugh, and even cry a little together. I hope you hang around, because I'm really looking forward to sharing this book with you.

I'm not saying that if you follow all this advice you are going to get married, but what I *am* saying is that this book consists of the 100 lessons I wish I would have known when I was still dating. It cost me a lot of time and heartache to find my wife and how we met was a complete surprise—but we'll get to that later.

Now, you probably know this already; but dating isn't easy.

Yeah, dating can be hard.

It's hard because we have to go on so many dates that will end in failure. Usually, when we fail at something over and over and over again, we give up; but not with dating. In fact—if you take out all of that "I learned a lot from the experience" stuff until you go out with your future spouse—every date could be considered a failure.

But it isn't just hard because of the failed dates we go on, but it's also hard because of all the dates we never go on. About a third of all the women I've asked out have said no, have canceled last minute, or have just plain stood me up.

So with all of these terrible dates we must go on and all of the rejection we have to go through to get to those terrible dates . . . why would we ever date?

Well, because while this thing called dating can be lonely, it can also be one of life's sweetest experiences. It is an awesome way to meet new people. It is an amazing way to learn more about yourself. It is an essential way to prepare for a great marriage.

Keep perspective on the positive. For while there have been hard times and tears in my dating life, most of it contains super fun memories with incredibly fun people.

And the most important reason why we should keep dating is because **dating never works . . . until it does.**

And it will.

WHY YOU'RE SINGLE

YOU DON'T STINK AT DATING, YOU'RE JUST A GOOD PERSON

I was talking to one of my friends about her dating life. She had been having a hard time.

And granted, she probably should have been.

After all, she really *was* a pretty bad dater.

"Zack," she said almost in tears, "I feel like there is a big neon sign on my head saying 'I STINK.' I don't know how to play the dating game. Can you teach me?"

As I was contemplating what I could say I had a realization that stung me to the core with honest introspection.

A lot of the things that make her really "bad" at dating . . . make her a really good spouse and parent.

She is genuine.

She puts time into her dates.

She throws her whole heart into any relationship.

She is committed.

She is generous.

She is kind.

A lot of the things that make someone "good" at dating . . . make for a really terrible spouse and parent.

They use manipulation.

They pretend to be too busy.

3

They hold back their emotions.

They keep options open.

They are selfishly physical.

They don't care.

Okay, so take a step back, "What is the *point* of dating?"

Now there are the things that people do along the way, but the end game, the honeypot of dating is . . . ?

Marriage.

And a good one, at that.

Let's stop playing the dating game. Let's start playing for keeps. Let's unlearn the dating game.

So what was my advice to her?

While she may not go on as many dates, may not be as good of a flirt, and may not *appear* to be as self-confident as others who are "professionals" at the dating game . . . she is much closer to marriage than any of them.

No, that "I STINK" sign certainly isn't for her (and I hope it's not for you either); it's for all the people who passed her by.

So if you are a good person, don't worry about being a bad dater.

Daters gunna date date date date date, just shake it off (please don't sue me, TS).

As for you . . . well, I'm pretty sure you're what marriage is for.

DON'T FEAR MARRIAGE—YOU CAN MAKE IT!

Right before I met my fiancée, I traveled . . . a lot.

My friends would tell me, "Get that all out of your system now, because when you're married . . ."

Then they would trail off into an assumed negative statement of common knowledge about how marriage means that life isn't fun or something.

Sure, it becomes more expensive and more difficult (especially with kids), but does excitement have to be drained out of a relationship because of family?

In pondering over that question, I realized **one of my biggest fears about marriage is that life will become audaciously ordinary, banal—dull.**

Of the couples I have observed, there are very few marriages that actually look enjoyable to me. (Now admittedly, the couples in those relationships may be perfectly content; it just doesn't seem like it would work for *me*. Maybe you've felt the same way as you've looked at marriages.) I'd say less than five percent of marriages look like something I can stomach.

Not great odds. But determined to beat the odds, I analyzed the commonalities between the marriages I admired.

There were two factors I've noticed in those five percent of marriages:

1. **They have respect for each other.** They are friends.
2. **They work for adventure.** Not that they spend thousands of dollars traveling, but they share new experiences with each other.

These couples have regular dinners together. They have jars they fill with money for their travels. They go out on picnics on the weekend. They have date nights. They celebrate each other. They play sports with each other on sunny days. They give high fives. They hold hands. They write notes of encouragement. They cook pancakes at midnight with all their kids. They live a full life.

And while that may not seem like what most are looking for, it is *the* thing I'm looking for. A life without respect and adventure? While some call it reality, I call it "my fear of marriage."

Now I understand that "living cannot be all crescendo; there must be some dynamic contrast" (Neal A Maxwell, "Patience," BYU Speeches, November 27, 1979) and enjoyment in marriage is often difficult when kids are sick, a miscarriage occurs, a parent dies, and so on. But that is because **marriage doesn't make you happy or sad—it simply magnifies your personal happiness and sadness.**

You don't have to change your LinkedIn bio to "Fat Naggy Boring Homebody" when you put a ring on it.

So, regardless if you are single or dating, figure out the common factors of those marriages you most respect, write them down, and commit yourself to working on those aspects of life right now. This will help you overcome any fears you might have about the idea of marriage.

YOU JUST HAVEN'T MET THEM YET (OR REALIZED IT)

I have a friend who was dating this guy for a couple of years. He was ready to pull the trigger, kill his single life, and propose; but my friend just couldn't get herself there. She always felt like something within was holding her back and trapping her heart.

So she tried to get herself out of her own prison.

She went to therapy to improve but was discouraged.

She read books about how to be exclusive but had eyes for others.

She prayed to get over her fears, but the thought of marriage was still scary.

Nothing worked.

Then . . . she finally dumped him.

She fed him the line, "It's not you, it's me" garbage and she honestly believed it.

He told her that she had crazy phobia of commitment and would stay single forever if she didn't fix herself.

But . . .

Two weeks later she met a guy, a month later she was engaged, and a few months later she was married.

She finally felt free. Turns out, she was trying to escape the wrong prison the whole time—it wasn't about the dark cage of dreadful commitment but the weary prison of the wrong person.

Now look, a lot of you are going to read that story and think that you are great and don't need to change and you just haven't met the right one.

Chances are, you do need some improvements.

But **when you meet someone who could be the right person, you *want* to change to make yourself a better you** (NOTE: not just a "better person," but a "better *you*").

When you meet someone you want to be with, guess what . . . ? *You want to be with them*! Your fearful outlook begins to change. Improving is encouraging, not a bummer. Being exclusive is a relief, not a sacrifice. Talks about the future together are exciting, not scary.

On the way to my wedding, I asked my then fiancée if she felt nervous. She didn't. Neither did I. Pretty weird coming from a guy who was accused of being a commitment-phobe my entire dating life.

But it wasn't scary. Actually, it was easy.

I wasn't afraid of commitment—I was afraid of commitment with the wrong person.

So if you are in a relationship and have worked at improving and getting over your fears and aren't sure why you still feel uneasy, try to walk away. It might give you the perspective to help you understand the source of your fear.

Because if you don't want to be with someone and are fearful about the relationship, **maybe it isn't you, but them *for* you. Finding a new "them" might be the key to make a free "you."**

GO ON DATES . . . BUT NOT TOO MANY—THE CANDY SHOP THEORY

Imagine you are a kid who was given five dollars and ten minutes to go into a candy store and pick out your favorite candy. Your tongue salivates and your nerve receptors start to trigger a chain reaction of excited bliss. You are told that you can try one piece of any candy you want, with the caveat that you can only spend the five dollars on *one* type of candy.

You are set loose.

You grab a jellybean, a sour straw, a Swedish fish, a chocolate kiss, a gummy bear, and a gumball. You shove them all in your mouth at the same time.

But that is just the start.

Before your teeth even clench for the first bite, both your hands are full again of confectionary concoctions that are continuously crammed into your face.

You haphazardly proceed in a state of mind where timelessness is your only reference to reality. Then you look at the clock.

Nine minutes are up.

What have you found? You can't possibly discern your favorite kind of candy; they all taste the same. One mound of delicious amazingness lost on a pallet drowned in gobs of sugar.

And here we so often find ourselves with dating.

It all kind of tasted the same.

When you are dating too many people at once, it becomes hard to differentiate. It truly isn't about how many dates, but the motivation behind the dates. It is hard to really get to know ten people at the same time.

So what is the number?

You have to decide for you—just make sure you have enough emotional bandwidth to give it an honest shot.

And what's the time frame?

Again, you have to decide for you—I recommend not getting serious too young and don't wait to get serious until too old.

Because when I stopped putting so much pressure on myself to choose *one* in a certain time frame through a frantic search, I realized I was happy. And I was floored with what I found, and you will be too—if you just breathe and give it a chance. Don't worry about any fake expiration dates you have. I used to tell my parents every Christmas that by next Christmas I would give then a daughter-in-law and that simply led to stressful summers trying to date too many people and frantic falls trying to get one to commit to me to hit my deadline.

Sure, I may have a canker sore or two, but I am happy because I've been exposed to a whole world outside of that one little shop and that brief ten minutes.

And you want to know the best part?

I've still got my five dollars . . .

TAKE THE CHALLENGE: BE A POPCORN DATER

In 2008, a group of friends sat me down for an intervention.

"Zack, you date like popcorn. Just bouncing around everywhere. We're going to give you a challenge."

They gave me a box with eight bags of Old Fashioned Natural popcorn and wrote on the box, "The possessor of this box, Zack Oates, agrees to go on eight separate dates with the same girl and on each date eat one bag of popcorn (one per date)" and made me sign it.

My roommates ate three bags without asking me over the years, so it was down to five.

Truth be told, I don't believe in going on movie dates (kissing) before a third date (until I met my wife, that is . . . #sorrynotsorry).

Needless to say (yet for some reason I'll still say it anyway), I didn't pop a single bag.

By the time I got married at the end of 2015, the five remaining bags were expired. *But* **the principle of focusing on going on dates with one person changed my mentality and is what enabled me to get married.**

Since we just talked about candy and candy + popcorn are the best couple ever to take to a movie (even if you're the third wheel), we're going to put this to the test.

Here is your challenge if you are really looking to get married (so this doesn't apply for high-school-aged readers):

Think of *one* person you are dating that you like the most or figure out someone you'd like to date. Now, hang out with them and then get them on a date. And then go on at least five dates in a row before you go out with anyone else. (To the younger readers I challenge you to only go on group dates before you graduate high school and never the same person twice in a row.)

Here's the thing—love, marriage, dating—they are all choices. A choice to be ready, a choice to be open, and then a choice to be committed.

Everyone is loved incredibly by someone. Use those five dates in a row to find out why they are loved so much.

Take the challenge and be a Popcorn Dater!

SETTLE DOWN, THERE *ARE* STILL GOOD PEOPLE

Look, Joan (or John) of Arc, sure you've had your heart ripped out and maybe you've had a bad streak of dating prospects. Maybe she cheated on you, maybe he was a jerk, maybe she was emotional, maybe he didn't care enough . . . and yeah, maybe that has been the story of your life for the last few attempts.

First of all, I'm sorry. That stinks. If you are really upset, just jump to the last few sections to see what to do about discouragement.

Okay, back?

Second of all, lift your head up from that dumped trash of your past and see that there is a bright future! There are amazing men and incredible women who are waiting for you!

There are single doctors that are humble and have great parents. There are Harvard MBAs with a desire to help orphans. There are also those who really like candy + popcorn and movie nights.

Good people still exist and to proceed in this epic revival of your next success, believe this: **Not all real men were killed off by dysentery on the Oregon Trail and not all ladies are married already to young tech millionaires.**

But the only way you'll see them is if you're looking.

So finish off that ice cream, change out of those PJs, and go find them. It might not be a conquest, but it sure will be a treasure.

Now, if you are one of those pieces of trash making dating miserable for everyone . . . then stay home. May your ice cream be melted and your PJs tangled forever.

THE BIG, FAT SINGLE LIE

You would never guess whom (yes, that still is a word) I bumped into after a breakup a few years ago . . .

It was at the end of a fourteen-hour hot workday outside. My face was still warm from the 105-degree Texas sun and my right eye was slightly twitching from the 5-Hour Energy I drank to get me through the last 30 minutes of the day (it was still barely enough). I stumbled into CVS looking for something—or someone . . . I wasn't sure.

Then, as I was meandering around, the way you do when you don't want to buy anything, but don't quite want to leave—I saw her.

Her sultry glare shared my sunken stare. She almost didn't recognize me. I can't blame her, though. I had earned an extra crease under both eyes since she last saw me a few months earlier. She was leaning against the candy aisle, eyeing the chocolate.

It was a vision of "my single life" . . .

I had been dreading this moment since becoming single again, but I knew it would come.

"Shall we? . . . For old time's sake?" she posed, motioning to a bag of peanut butter M&M's.

Somehow, I think she knew I would come back to her.

"You know," I stammered as I awkwardly ran my fingers through my hair, "I didn't really mean all those things I said when I left you . . . that last time."

She knew I was lying. After all, I lied every other time I dragged myself and 22 candy-coated grams of sugar back to her.

She saw me glance at the fun pack. With her condescendingly cheap chuckle, she picked up the king size bag and tossed it to me.

"It's Saturday night. Do you have plans?"

She can be so cruel.

In a flash I could see her wearing a wedding dress . . . weighing 500 diabetes-enabled pounds (say "no" to that dress, please!).

And for the first time in my life I truly realized the big fat single lie was right (wrong) in front of me:

Being single isn't as glamorous as it would seduce you to believe and being in a relationship isn't as bad as it appears from a surface level.

See, the single life will lure you in with promises of fun, freedom, and more fun. *Hot tub until your forehead gets pruney* (by yourself), *vacation until you run out of ideas* (money), *and never ask for permission* (because no one cares). But she'll never tell you that the heated water, adventure, excitement, and fun can be had without her. She won't mention that when you enjoy life with another, you have the freedom of compound happiness.

Compound happiness is when you get even happier when you're happy knowing that you being happy makes someone else happy, and them being happier makes you even happier.

She will veil the truth behind the ivory web of lies that she weaves so carefully . . . concealing her make-ups for markdowns from the forethought exams. Even with life's lemons in the limelight of her limited outlook, she fails to look within herself. For if she did, she would see a bitter hollow shell.

For with her, there isn't eternal support, kind words, sweet notes, meaningful kisses, gentle reminders, someone to think about during chick flicks, a well of intensely personal advice, a loving ear or a willing heart. She will try to convince you that by jumping in your ride and heading out tonight riding solo is YOLO, but know that the ice cream, Ambien, and Netflix cocktails can't drown the innate desire of a human to care about and be cared about on a plane that is higher than platonic friendship. Ah yes, what she offers pales in comparison to what she never can give . . .

In the middle of my marriage mirage (perhaps energy-drink induced), I was interrupted by an employee telling me that they were closing up.

Wow, I thought, *my first Saturday night single in almost a year and I made last call . . . at CVS.*

I slid by my slyly stubborn single seductress and snagged six bags of chocolate. Just enough for one . . . because I knew that, at least for that night, no one would carry me home. (Not) fun.

But . . . I soon realized the truth of the saying "this too shall pass." You'll be able to dump your single life forever and embark on a journey of a lifetime—and yes, it will be sweet.

DATING FUNDAMENTALS

MEN ARE ATTRACTED ON POINTS— WOMEN ON SPECTRUMS

To get you started, here are a few things that are worth knowing about dating:

Men find women attractive on a point.

Women find men attractive on a spectrum.

To illustrate, I'm going to use the 10-point attractiveness scale.

Here's how it works: If a guy sees a girl and thinks she is a solid 8, that is usually where she stays. She could be suuuuper sweet and nice and spiritual and intelligent and that might kick her up to an 8.5. She could be bat tart crazy and that would bump her down to a 7.5. But that first impression is hard to move very much. **Hence, men find women attractive on a point.**

Now for women . . . oh no. This is where things get interesting. When a woman meets a man, she may rate him, say, a 7—but some women won't even rate a guy at all in the beginning! They will just somehow suspend rating until more data has been collected. Then, when she does decide that he is a 7, that is just an *anchor* of a range. The algorithm that goes into the *real* number has been studied by men the ages over (that is actually how Google started), but is yet undiscovered. It could be the moon cycle, the weather, the day, the things the guy just said/

did/wore/wrote/posted/texted, her work schedule, her hair, her roommates, and on and on. So that 7 could be a 2 or a 9 on any given day at any given time. (Now there is one exception and that is a man in a well-tailored bespoke suit . . . but that is for another topic.) Hence, **women find men attractive on a spectrum.**

So what does that mean for all of us?

Well for girls, it means you just do you and let the guy fall into the right place.

For guys . . . it means good luck and get humble because if you're a 9, no one knows how you got there and you probably won't be there for long.

But in the end, we need to remember that **in the process of finding love, we look for our 10s by finding our 7s and making them our 1.**

FIVE BASIC MESSAGES DECODED

These are a few ideas for decoding some not-so-subtle messages hidden in plain sight. This is for women, who often will turn puddles into oceans, and for men, who . . . well they have trouble getting in any kind of water.

DODGING RESCHEDULING THE DATE DECODER

When she says, "Shoot, I'm super busy!" (and no "*but* when else can we get together . . .") she's really saying, "Things would be different if you would have just used that gym pass of yours more."

When he says, "We should do this again," (and doesn't ask when you're free) he's really saying, "I'm not so sure we should do this again."

BEFORE THE DATE DECODER

When she says "I'm running late, can you pick me up an hour later?" she's really saying "We won't make out tonight."

When he says, "Where do you want to eat?" he's really saying, "Please just pick any place close and not too expensive because I was too busy to really plan this date out and don't want to go somewhere too nice or I would have called for reservations."

TESTING THE WATER QUESTIONS DECODER

When she says, "Do you think our kids would be attractive?" she's really saying, "You've never thought about our kids, I hope."

When he says, "So how many boys have you kissed?" he's really saying, "Can we add one more to your list tonight?"

CUTE TEXT DECODER

When she says, "You are awesome ;-)," she's really saying "I just really wish you were as awesome as my last boyfriend who is dating that trash right now, but you're not—so you'll do. But I guess that, really, you aren't that bad. . . . So I'll put a smiley face to make you think it was sincere, but I'll make it a winky face so you know I'm kinda joking."

When he says, "I've been thinking about you all day," he's really saying "I've been pretty bored."

BREAKING UP DECODER

When she says, "I'm not sure I feel the spark," she's really saying, "You're an idiot."

When he says, "I'm not sure where this is going," he's really saying, "I know exactly where this is going."

IF THEY SET YOU UP WITH A FRIEND, IT IS *NOT* GOING WELL

So I went on a date with this girl.

Beautiful, spiritual, smart, positive . . . everything I could ask for (this technically should be "for which I could ask," but colloquialism will take precedent over correctness here).

Things were going smoothly—maybe even a kiss by the end of the night, who knew?

It was a beautiful evening. The secluded beachfront hot tub set just the right mood at the end of the date. The stars were beaming down in faultless splendor. And right as cheesy lines were spinning through my head of how to not mess up this perfect evening . . .

Things turned sour.

Like "mouthful of rotten ocean water" sour.

She goes, "You know, I think you and Alicia would be such a great couple!"

[Silence]

[Furrow eyebrows]

[Left eye slightly squint in confusion]

[A little more silence]

"What did you just say?" The question could barely leave my lips after that sucker-punch to the ego.

"No, I mean, I just think that you guys would be great for each other."

I couldn't help it. I started to laugh.

Not like the "oh this is funny," laugh, but like the "I'm getting a shot at the doctor and don't know what else to do" kind of laugh.

"Well, I guess there isn't any pressure for the rest of this date then, is there?" I mused to myself out loud.

"I think you're a great guy and all, but . . ."

The rest was, as they say, the story of my life.

Yes, a telltale sign that you are as burnt as forgotten toast is if your date ever mentions you dating someone else.

If you've had this used on you, you're not alone.

But if you've pulled this one, please use this tactic wisely and rarely. Oh . . . and you're a coward.

DATING IS LIKE PASSING GAS— IF YOU TRY TOO HARD, IT HURTS

I have a philosophy when dating . . . it is called not trying too hard. Again, this is a philosophy and works in theory, but it's a little harder in practice (like communism and lettuce wraps with extra dressing . . . both sound good but are, in reality, a disaster).

The problem is this: you don't just have to find *a someone* whom you like; but they have to actually like you. (Cue gasp of self-realization [BWAHHH?] . . . and we're back.)

I see this statistical anomaly prove itself out in every decent marriage. Getting a good guy to like a good girl . . . and having that *same* good girl liking that good guy. (Why can't we just go back to how it used to be in having the girl settling for the guy?)

But in the end folks, even though I've heard mixed reviews about it, I believe in marriage. (Take a deep breath for this next run-on sentence) I believe that two people can fall madly in love and sift that fairy-tale feeling up through the raging sands of reality to settle on top as a polished stone of true joy, where the "happily ever after" will be something two mortals are working towards and not a finished product.

And on this quest to find that right arithmetic fit of an unquantifiable *i*, it really is tough to not try too hard. Sometimes you can't help but wonder if a girl can be a future wife on a first date, or if the guy will be a good dad on the second or what a third date would look like when saying "hi" to someone . . . but with something so important, how can I tell you not to try too hard? It's totally understandable.

I can only say this: if you are going to try hard, **don't try hard to impress someone else, but try hard to be authentically you.**

Don't worry why they waited an extra five minutes to text you back, but just be grateful you are texting. Enjoy the process and try not to get caught up in the details.

For if you have patience, I think you'll find that there are more people looking to "settle down and step up" than there are people looking for too much red dressing.

HOW TO KNOW IF YOU'RE BEING TOO PICKY . . . AND ROBOTS

I dropped by my old roommate's apartment to catch up after not seeing him for a couple of weeks.

He saw me walk in and without even making eye contact asked, "So how are things going with that one girl?" His half-smirk hinted at his undeniable undertones of subtle scoffing.

I knew he had no idea who that "one girl" was, but after knowing me for a few years, he just assumed there was some "one girl."

I pretended to not notice his gentle jab.

"Eh . . . you know how things go. It didn't work out. She—"

"What was wrong with this one?" The facetious flavor became more pronounced (by the way, "facetious" is one of over 20 words in the English language that uses all of the vowels once in alphabetical order . . . just in case you get nothing out of this section, here is at least one thing).

He got a little more to the point while looking up from his book. "I think you are too picky."

My response for the previous six years was that I was not picky, I just wanted someone with whom I could fall in love. Not too much to ask . . . right?

Right.

Well . . . unless of course you are only willing to fall in love with perfection.

I had ended things with so many amazing girls just "because . . ."

And in looking back at the things I haven't liked about girls, it has included traits like being too young, too old, too nice, not nice enough, too serious, too immature, too skinny, not skinny enough, too concerned with fashion, not good style, weird friends, messy, plain, quirky, too busy, too available, and on and on. Now if one person had all of those traits, then yeah, maybe we could look elsewhere (like to a shrink).

But chances are, I never gave never actually gave girls a chance after a first date because of some minor perceived "flaw." Maybe I exacerbated-ly extrapolated her quietness into something that would be the grounds for divorce or a broken home or a miserable life every time I came home from work and then I would be bored when we were sitting in our rocking chairs watching our great-grandkids just sit in the yard like idiots looking at the grass grow because they learned how to be dull from my wife.

Well slo-o-o-o-o-o-o-o-o-w down there, Tonto! It's just a first date . . .

And therein is the problem. We feel justified when, if we notice something in the beginning we don't like, we fail to give them another chance. But if we are feeling off for a night, we expect them to give us another chance.

The more someone dates, the more they realize what is so great about other people. We begin to form this Captain Planet as an assimilation of the powers of all your previous relationships combined. See, I've dated the perfect girl for service, the perfect girl for beauty, the perfect girl for spirituality, the perfect girl for intellect, the perfect girl for cocktail parties, and so on . . . but they were all different girls. I would never find someone who possesses all of those qualities and hope that that someone wouldn't expect me to possess them as well.

As a recovering perfection-aholic, might I suggest a simple phrase to keep in mind? A phrase that we expect others to believe about us, but that we rarely exercise in our perception of others:

Give them the benefit of the doubt—until they give you reason enough to doubt the benefit.

And there it is.

So does perfect exist? Yeah, of course it does . . . just not in one person and most certainly not in ourselves. We will never find a match who is perfect, but we can find a perfect match. And because that match isn't perfect, we don't have to marry a robot.

See, what I didn't quite realize back then was that I'm going to date, marry, and live with a human for the rest of my life. A human not only who has faults, but also who can live with mine. And while robots might be perfect, there are better things: humans. For with all of their flaws, pet peeves, laziness, loudness, quietness, and rudeness . . . only humans, imperfect humans, are capable of love.

THE FRIEND ZONE

ARE YOU PUTTING YOURSELF IN THE FRIEND ZONE?

I'm going to put this out there: that "friend" that you are crushing on and aren't sure if it is the right time and are worried about taking things farther because you might "ruin the friendship" . . . you know that one?

It's time.

Drop that crush like a Twinkie addiction (#RIPHostess).

The risk of "ruining the friendship" is poppycock. Think about it. In three years you are either going to be married or not talking because no one's spouse likes them chilling with their former crush that they wish they dated but never had the chutzpah to do it (and if you haven't heard of "chutzpah," you probably didn't grow up in Jersey. But now you have, so welcome to the club).

Until the chill steel blade of "I'm so glad we're friends" leaves their lips, there is still time to interrupt them with yours.

I have a friend that used to be fat. Not just fat, but, like, insecure and fat. He never put himself out there for girls because he never thought he could get them. Well, he decided to shed some weight and he got stylish and he started getting lots of attention.

But while his body changed, his confidence didn't.

He never went after girls, he just always asked them about their dating lives and did brunch (and he was straight).

I would tell him, "You aren't a fat kid anymore. Be more than friends."

And while it isn't easy at times for him, he will get through it because he is one of the greatest guys I've ever met (imagine if Mother Theresa and Willy Wonka raised a kid together—that's him).

And so it is emotionally with us. We need to give ourselves the credit to lay down those bad habits and remember that **if you never leave the safety of the friend zone, you'll never have anything but friends.**

SIX WAYS TO KNOW THAT YOU ARE THE STRAIGHT GAY BEST FRIEND

I was trying to date this girl. I had tried the year before, and even the year before that. So third time is a charm(ing disaster), right?

It was actually our fourth date in two weeks. Seemed like it was going well.

But I wasn't so sure because she wasn't being as physical as I thought she would be. Not the kind you're thinking about, but there was no forearm touch with head tossed back in slightly superfluous laughter, no leg graze with an eye gaze, not even an extended hand grab to get my attention. *Zippp.*

Then, the moment she opened her front door for our fourth date it hit me like a ton of multicolored bricks: we weren't dating.

I was her straight gay best friend. "Zack," you might be saying, "come on now. How could you tell that from just looking at her?"

The giveaway: she was wearing crocs.

I mean crocs.

On a date.

Crocs?!?!?!

Not gardening.

Not showering outside a jungle tent.

Not dressing up for Halloween as People of Walmart . . .

On a date.

When she threw on a wrinkled collared shirt to go with her yoga pants, I really couldn't hide my facial expression anymore.

"What's wrong?" she probed.

"Ummm, did you just want to go to the drive-through?"

She started to laugh. I awkwardly chuckled . . . still waiting for a response.

Although I tried to ask her out again just in case, she declined, realizing my intentions were not to go shopping with her.

I eventually forwent (apparently that is a real word) the white flag and raised a rainbow flag in surrender. I moved on.

So how can you know if you are dating or just a straight gay best friend? These six giveaways will get you started:

1. If she wears crocs [sigh].
2. If she invites you to pick out jeans with her.
3. If she asks you to bring her Cherry Garcia ice cream.
4. If she asks you to watch any Nicholas Sparks book turned movie.
5. If she says, "We should get pedis!"
6. And the killer . . . if she asks you for guy advice.

MEN—If you are in the straight gay best friend zone . . . don't worry, it isn't a shot at your masculinity, but an assertion that you will get along well with your future wife.

WOMEN—If you have put a guy in the straight gay best friend zone . . . hate to break it to you, but you are a terrible person. (Okay, you're not a terrible person, but you are wasting his time. He doesn't want to be friends with you even if he thinks he wants to be friends with you. No one likes being just friends with their crush—oh, and that "one guy" isn't the exception.)

Now, if you are a gay guy, would you *please* set up your straight guy friends? You have so many hot girl friends.

FOUR STEPS TO STAY OUT OF THE FRIEND ZONE

Maybe they're out of your league.

Maybe you're scared of rejection.

. . . Or maybe everyone just assumes you're asexual.

Whatever the reason, you've gone and done it.

You've taken a perfectly good dating prospect and friend zoned them. You put the quarantine signs of "Radioactively Unavailable" in your yard and no amount of milk shake is going to bring the boys (or girls) back.

I received an email a while ago from a young lady who has spent so long friend-zoning every eligible male around her that she cannot help but come to the realization that the cats of single-hood are scraping at her door.

She asked me what she should do.

So I looked at the times in my life and my close friends' lives when they have been able to get out of the friend zone and I put together four steps to stay out of the friend zone. There are two STOPs and two STARTs.

1. STOP talking about other relationships. I had a dear friend who was one of the most internally and externally attractive people on the face of this earth. We would always talk about each other's interests until one day I told her that I was done talking about other relationships and thought that we should just have one ourselves. While it didn't go over that well . . . at least I wasn't wasting either of our times. Which brings me to my next point . . .

2. STOP pretending you will stay friends. It is *possible* on *rare* occasions after marriage to have friends of former interests because there is always an exception, but I can safely say—you're not it.

3. START believing you deserve more. You have to first believe that you *can* get them and deserve it. None of this self-pity. You deserve to be treated well and feel lucky.

4. START showing interest. Flirt, get them to ask you out (girls) or ask them out (boys), put in a movie and cuddle . . . or just, ya know . . . kiss them. Seriously. It works super well (sometimes, for some people).

Now if they still don't respond, remember the golden rule: either they aren't interested or they are too dumb for you to have kids with . . . and nobody needs that.

So this is your friendly reminder to start breaking and stop building that front yard fence of friendship . . . milk shakes optional.

DUMP THE FRIEND ZONE WITH A RANDOM KISS

"And then . . . she just kissed me."

We have all been there.

We like someone but aren't sure to the extent that we like them so it remains in this lukewarm awkward phase where nothing will bake until someone turns up the heat in a dramatic way. And if you can't handle the heat, you're out of the kitchen.

See, I liked this girl, but the tempestuous taskmaster of time had not put us on the same proverbial shift. I was interested when she was occupied, she was intrigued when I was unavailable.

After eons (in single-standard time) of back and forth, we were finally single at the same time . . . but the feelings were so . . . odd. After years of maintaining a pseudo-friend-based relationship built on future expectations and "what ifs," it was just so bizarre. I felt like a kid who was given cupcakes and chocolate frosting and told to go decorate them in the off-limits sitting room reserved only for formal guests.

It was just too much.

We went out, baked, talked, texted, and did everything that you are supposed to do when you like someone . . . but I just couldn't bring myself to actually pull a move.

But my over-analytical abilities were kind enough to give me the jitters, get me nervous, and push my heart out of the potential kill zone. Buuuuuuuut, I still hung out with her.

Recipe for disaster.

Yup. I was that guy.

Well one day, this frazzled girl, perplexed by my peculiar conduct, had enough. She called me told me to come outside where she was parked in front of my house.

I complied.

She opened her door and as I went to give her a hug, she grabbed my face, pushed me up against the car, and kissed me.

I mean she really kissed me.

For the first time since I could remember . . . I . . . was . . . speechless.

Like. . . . Nothing.

After about 20 blinks, I looked down and saw that I had an ice cream pop in my hand. I merely held it up and said, "So . . . do you want the rest of this?"

While we ended up chatting and figuring that things wouldn't work out, I have seen this same technique end with fantastically positive results (and in this girl's case it probably did).

But I will always respect a person who is willing to put themselves out to see if there is a way out of the friend zone death spiral. Because when you pull a move like that, it is either going to bake the cake or turn the oven off. Either way, you leave the friend zone and enter either a true friendship or a semi-sweet bitterness. But hey, at least you don't have to wait to find out.

BEFORE THE DATES

FIVE STEPS TO MAKE YOUR "LIST"

I've always believed that I didn't want someone to be the wind beneath my wings nor someone who would bring me along as cargo, but rather someone who can fly with me. That sounds nice and all, but what does that actually mean?

Right before I met my wife, I made a list to figure it out. It helped to clear my mind and, in large measure, is the reason we worked out!

But before we get into making a list, there are two stories that are absolutely critical to read.

STORY ONE

I have a friend who was dating this guy.

She really liked him, but couldn't quite figure out if it was worth going to the next level, so she wrote out a list of pros and cons. There were some really good things about him, but just some stuff that bugged her too. *If only he could change these things*, she thought.

Then, she actually prayed to find out what else she might be missing. She felt prompted to open up her scriptures to a random verse and what she read hit her right between the eyes.

"Why beholdest thou the mote that is in thy brother's eye, but considerest not the beam that is in thine own eye? Thou hypocrite, first cast out the beam out of thine own eye" (Matthew 7:3–5).

Bam. #BibleSlap

STORY TWO

I had my buddy write out all of the things he wanted in a wife. After reciting a long list, I read it back to him and he nodded in agreement.

Then I asked him if that list described him.

He didn't even need to think about it.

The answer was no.

THE FIVE STEPS

You might be like me, when, after reading these stories, I could give a tisk-tisk Dikembe Mutombo finger wag and think of a few friends who should read this section.

But I would encourage you to fight against the urge of thinking of others and **take a fresh batch of humble pie to realize that so often in life, we underestimate others while overestimating ourselves**. We find the fallible in others and excuse the errors in ourselves by feigning good intentions.

Is it wrong to make a list? *No!*

But make sure you include **all** these steps:

1. Think of the people you wish you could marry/date and think about what you respect most about them. Write it down.
2. Think of your exes and why you broke up. Write down the opposite.
3. Write down the things you love most about your best friends, coolest roommates, closest family members, and think about what allows you to click so well with them.
4. Choose *only* five must-haves and five nice-to-haves. Put the others aside for review later. Keep in mind that when you truly love someone, they *become* your list.
5. Make those attributes **your personal goals.**

So right now, before you even read the next section, make a list and check it twice . . . but make sure the second time is for yourself.

And as far as flying goes . . . remember, you don't attract a swan by acting like a penguin.

KINDNESS IS THE *MOST* IMPORTANT TRAIT FOR YOUR LIST

So you made your list.

Wait . . . you haven't?

Just give it a try for five minutes and then come back.

Seriously.

Okay, welcome back . . . so think about it: what is the sexiest attribute to have on your list?

What is the attribute that really makes a human super?

To me, there is *one* singular attribute that takes the wedding cake on sexiness.

This attribute isn't hotness, spirituality, ambition, passion, cleverness, brilliance, skinniness . . .

It is authentic kindness.

I have a best friend who looks like Thor. He described authentic kindness to me as how a person treats someone who can do nothing for them.

Yeah . . . seriously.

That is it. Didn't need his hammer to nail that definition.

Authentic kindness.

Once, I asked my grandpa why he and my grandma, who passed a few years earlier, had such an amazing marriage. Without hesitation, other than to hold back some soft tears, he said, "It was your grandmother's kindness. When we would argue, she was so quick to forgive and so kind to me. That is what held our marriage together and made me a better person."

There is nothing that could make a better wife, husband, mother, father, or (super) human being than authentic kindness.

I have a friend who is very pretty. Then one day she became incredibly beautiful. I saw her talking to a very anti-social, rude person at a party and I was going to go over and "save" her, but I realized that she was there by choice. She spent the whole party at this person's side to make sure that they were having a good time and felt included. This person was not someone that she ever would have dated, but she never once broke eye contact to see if people were watching her. She just genuinely is a kind person who cared about this child of God.

Kindness is not being concerned with what you get out of the interaction.

Kindness is optimistic and positive with the thoughts and dreams of others.

Kindness is the most important superpower that anyone can have (even Thor).

And yeah, kindness is super sexy.

IT'S OKAY TO HANG OUT . . . WITH DISCRETION

That's right, I'd like to make a case for hanging out.

Now before you gather the pitchforks . . . hear me out.

I'm not saying don't date.

I'm just saying that "hanging out" has unjustly become a curse word (. . . or phrase?).

Men and women should go on one-on-one dates.

But we need to go on dates for the right reasons.

Many have dated for years, but the relationship clock never struck "marriage time," not because the gears weren't working, but because they were working too hard.

See, when we date, we are trying to be the best we can be and, quite frankly, we are trying to find the worst in the other person.

Yes, dating is essentially trying to impress while looking for deal breakers.

When we hang out, we are usually calm, casual, and quite frankly, a little more realistically ourselves.

Some of the best relationships I've seen have started with a friendship (while avoiding the friend zone).

Those friendships were not forged in the fires of flirtation, but rather built on the basis of a casual closeness. When in hot pursuit, you rarely are going to chill out and be totally yourself, but rather you try to be what you think they want you to be.

When hanging out, there are no expectations, so you can just be you and they can just be them.

So don't fear the dessert parties of hanging out, but be aware to not deny yourself of the hearty dinners of dating. Both, coupled (pun intended—tehehe) together, will create a strong bond that will withstand the mob of your single life wanting more dessert.

MAKE YOUR CHICKEN LIST . . . THEN *DO IT*!

You aren't chicken.

You are awesome.

So prove it.

Make a list of the top five people you would like to date and start going down the list. Guys, ask out the ladies starting at the top. Ladies, get the guy to ask you out (described in later sections).

Work your way down the list one by one until things work out or don't. When you get to the bottom, start again with a new list.

But buyer beware, you might not make it down the list. My buddy wrote out his chicken list and married his number one.

Try it, right now. Here is space for your top five.

1)

2)

3)

4)

5)

Now pull out your phone and do something about it.

What . . . are you chicken?

IF YOU FEAR, YOU LOSE

So there was a girl who had been interested in me. She made it clear (by telling me that she was interested) and seemed perfect, but I was just too afraid.

After a few months of not talking, I decided I would right my foolish indecision and groundless fear.

I called her.

Ring. Ring. Ring . . . she answered. First good sign (and last one of this story).

"Umm . . . hello?" she questioned.

"*Hey* there, stranger!

[Insert slightly awkward small talk.]

"So. The reason for my call."

"Yeah," she replied with tepidly confused anticipation.

"I was calling to say that I'm sorry. I was stupid and think you are amazing and there is nothing more I could possibly want than you. I don't want to date other people. I will do what I need to do to prove that I'm being sincere. I will fly out to you, I will make time every day for you, I will even quit Cheetos Puffs because—"

"Zack . . ."

Silence.

"It has been a while," she said with a sigh.

"I know, but—"

"I'm engaged."

It was as if a chilled steak knife cut out a raw piece of my heart.

I have an older friend who never got married. Once, she tearfully told me that her biggest regret in life was being too afraid to tell her crush that she was interested until he moved away to live closer to his soon-to-be wife. He regrettably confessed his feelings for her too, but it was too late.

It comes down to this: **lose your fear or lose your chance.**

FIVE STEPS TO START A CONVERSATION WITH ANYONE OF THE OPPOSITE GENDER

I walked up to a woman at a party doing my best (worst) to look cool and sly.

"Fat penguin."

I raised my eyebrows twice.

"What??" Her confusion was calculated to perfection.

"I just wanted to say something to break the ice!"

". . . ?"

"Get it? Penguins that are fat . . . ice breaking. Conversation ice breakers? Get it?"

She walked away.

So things don't always work and I'm certainly not an advocate for pickup lines. But I'll give you one question that has worked in almost every situation to start a casual conversation.

STEP One: Make eye contact with your target.

STEP Two: Look away with a slightly confused expression.

STEP Three: Make eye contact again.

STEP Four: Walk over with a smile.

STEP Five: Ask, "Who do people say you look like?"

And there it is. Everyone has heard they look like someone, so just use that as a jumping off point and start to get to know them. Oh, and if you meet that ONE girl who said she has never heard she looks like anyone, don't say she looks like Rosie O'Donnell . . . even if you clarify you meant the young attractive version from *A League of Their Own*. Apparently, that isn't a compliment.

Trust me.

YOU'RE NOT A 10, BUT YOU CAN STILL HAVE CONFIDENCE

So when it comes to looks, I'll be the one to break it to you: you're not a 10.

It's okay.

Own it.

Yeah, own who you are.

If you are a 7 or 6—great! *Own it.* Be that 7 and know that you are the best looking and coolest 7 in the whole room. That will instill confidence so that no matter what line you use, you will be speaking as an honest 7. Arrogance is thinking you're a 10, confidence is loving yourself as a 7. You can look at yourself and ask all day what the mirror, mirror on the wall thinks, or you can be honest, own it, and the rest will inevitably follow.

WOMEN HAVE BABIES; MEN OPEN DOORS

There is a misconception from some feminists that chivalry is dead. These are the same feminists, mind you, who are trying to kill it.

See, chivalry occurs when a gentleman decides to treat a lady right and the lady accepts the service.

On a date, a man should

1. Open doors
2. Walk on the street-side of the sidewalk
3. Did I mention to open doors?
4. Make her feel special
5. Pay

A woman should

1. Accept the chivalry

When it comes down to it, women bear children and hence, men are eternally indebted to them. While no amount of gentlemanly deeds will replace that, it does open the door to a healthy truth: it isn't which gender is better, but it is about truly believing there is a team, with each player having equal importance.

PAY ATTENTION TO YOUR DATE

My friend Brandon met this girl in class. She was cute and always sat on his left side (an important tidbit).

He asked her out. They went out. It was winter. She wore a coat. All things to this point seem normal.

Now here we go.

On their first date at his apartment, they sat (again, her at his left) at his computer watching some YouTube stuff to have a reason to sit close, touch knees, and kill some time (ya know the routine). As they sat, he couldn't help but notice that she was incredibly proficient at typing with one hand while the other stayed in her coat pocket.

Then, as they were making sandwiches, she still only used her right hand.

He started to laugh.

"Why do you only use one hand?" he blurted with a chuckle.

An uncomfortable silence ensued. The chuckle stopped.

"Because," she replied, "it's the only one I have."

Now there is nothing awkward about having one arm, but being friends with a girl for a few weeks and not noticing until (what turned out to be) the end of a date . . . now that can be awkward.

Needless to say, they did not go out again.

Let's just say this: pay attention to your interest. Look them in the eye, be sensitive to them, and always look at things from their perspective.

And please, for all that is worth a first kiss, put away your stupid phone.

In the end though, what I learned from this story is that it just goes to show you that there is at least ONE situation where getting a side hug at the end of a date doesn't necessarily mean you're out of luck . . . unless you're Brandon.

LOSING THE VISION OF BLIND DATES

I got a text from a buddy.

"Zack, can you set me up on a blind date?"

I thought for a couple of minutes, made a call and pulled off a miracle. They hit it off and got married! Yeah . . . so that's a complete lie and has never happened to me before, but I can imagine that it has happened for someone.

I have never had a single blind date end up in anything but me staying single. But what a blind date does do is it allows us to remain open to the possibility of love. The more you put yourself out there for the universe to prove that you are willing to take chances for the chance of love, the more those chances come your way.

Did I turn down a date from an ex-girlfriend's mother's sister's friend whose friend's daughter had just become single? No.

Did it go anywhere? No.

But we did become great friends.

So remember to always be looking to set up your friends and never take offense to the set up.

THE SEVEN *D'S* OF DATING DESPITE DIVORCE

"Hey, so I don't mean for this to be awkward, but can I ask you a personal question?"

I had met this woman a few days earlier and knew that she had been married, but a mutual friend wasn't sure if she was divorced. Say what you will, but I always kept a strict "no married, no exceptions" rule.

What added to the slight awkwardness of this phone call was that I was supposed to pick her up for our date in an hour.

"Sure!" she bounced back.

"So are you actually divorced or just separated?"

"Oh . . . [stammer] . . . well I called the court today and the papers are in the mail. [Silence] So as of this morning I'm divorced!"

"Cool! I'll pick you up soon."

So we went to a restaurant . . .

Where she cried about her ex. (Understandably)

Our second date was postponed . . . indefinitely.

So how do you get back into dating after a divorce, or just even a serious breakup? How do you actually put yourself out there again after going through one of the most awful experiences of your life?

Granted, I've never been divorced, so I had a few divorced friends help me write these seven rules.

1. **Don't Rush.** Time is based on heart, not calendar. Don't say that you will date in two months or two years . . . just pray every day to be ready to date and then give yourself the time you need.

2. **Dress Well!** Work from the outside in. The first thing one of my friends did was go out shopping with one of the straight gay best friends and got all new clothes (no crocs). She had been reduced to "mom jeans" and that just did not show off her curvy personality well enough.

3. **Date with *Zero* Expectations.** You just had your heart broken, give yourself a breath and don't try to think if this is your new baby's daddy. Just enjoy the ride.

4. **Don't Disqualify.** Beware of the "I hate guys/girls" syndrome. Know that not everyone is your ex. Give people a chance—especially yourself. Just make sure to keep to your top five list.

5. **Deserve Love.** Be *confident*! You are beautiful, handsome and wonderful and deserve to fall in love . . . yes, even again.

6. **Destroy Discouragement.** Realize it ain't easy! It's okay to be hurt and know that things aren't going to always work out, but in the end they will.

7. **Date!** Yeah . . . actually do it. Get your kids a babysitter, stop making excuses, and date. Ladies, flirt. Gentlemen, ask.

The biggest frustration I've heard is that it is so hard to trust your judgment. One of my dear friends who went through a terrible divorce (as if there is any other kind) said, "It is like my fire alarm didn't go off the first time and it is hard to trust it again." I told her that she knows what heat feels like now.

Just take your time and trust that you can do it.

Dating is a fun adventure—an adventure that is always there when you are ready to embark.

WHAT WOMEN WANT MEN TO KNOW

GUYS, DON'T BE TOO FORWARD

*H*onesty.
    Works great in relationships.
    Works great in chick-flicks.
    Works terribly at the end of a first date.
Story time.

I was on a date with a beautiful girl. I was shocked that she was even on the date with me and by the end of the date, so was she.

When I went to drop her off at the doorstep I said, "I just feel a real spark with us so I'm just going to warn you . . . I'm going to fight for you. I think we have a great thing going together and we can really make this work. I see a real future with us. My chest is just burning thinking about it."

It took her two years to talk to me again.

There is a wise proverb in, well funnily enough, Proverbs 29:11, "A fool uttereth all his mind, but a wise man keepeth it in till afterwards."

So before you dismount your white stallion to save your princess, know that chances are, she doesn't need saving. You need to give it time, space, and an equal amount of interest that she shows you.

There is a section about the Three-Point Rule coming up. Read it. A couple of times.

In Boy Scouts we learn that a great way to smother a good fire is too much firewood too soon. If you want to give the spark a chance, air is the best ingredient.

So too with the fires of love. A smothered fire will leave you cold and in the dark.

[Insert your own positive ending here.]

JERKS GET THE LADIES ONLY TEMPORARILY

I pursued this girl who was great. I mean super attractive, amazing resume, very funny—any guy would be ready to date her in an instant!

But then small things started to show a lack of interest, such as texting *on* a date with me, not calling back soon, and then making slightly demeaning comments. I asked around a little and found out that she was still interested in an old fling.

So when I started to see her backing away, I decided to perform a social experiment. I wanted to play the game. And not just like a foursquare "win or lose we all had fun" type of game, but more like the Mayan ball game where I would either be crowned a hero or die.

This is what happened: I told her I would show up at her house at nine p.m. on Sunday. I showed up at nine forty-five. I didn't even hug her when I walked in. I was rude. I teased her. I flirted with her roommates. I tasted her cookie dough and pretended I wasn't impressed. I even stuck a stick into the dough just to make a point that I could.

I was just a "class A" jerk and left in less than 30 minutes feeling like a total fool.

I really did feel bad. This totally was not my style at all. The only solace I had was knowing that this was my last ditch effort to get her.

I confessed to my roommates what I had done and in the midst of them lecturing me about why I shouldn't have done that, I get my first ever unsolicited text from her. *BWHA?!*

She wanted to get together that week for a date and a weekend road trip. *BWAAAAAAAAAAAAAH???????!* (Frankly, I was more disgusted that it worked than anything.)

She called me the next day to make sure that we were going out that week and that I could still make the weekend trip.

We went out.

We went out again and even again.

It was great, but she lost interest in me as I lost interest in playing the game . . . and she sacrificed me yet again on her altar of unanswered texts.

So . . . what is the moral of the story?

Fellas, **if the only way you can get her is to play crazy games, you never had her. You can't get a girl to like you by not being you!**

But yes, we need to play a little bit of the game, but play the right game. The game is not making it TOO obvious when you are interested.

The game is about intrigue, not injury.

So don't be that guy. Don't play the nasty games. Don't put up with those games.

You are better than that and you deserve someone who will think the same.

GIRLS GO FOR BAD BOYS BECAUSE GOOD GUYS ARE IDIOTS

"Girls never give us 'good guys' a chance and always end up with those 'bad boys' . . . ugh!"

If this is something some half-man has said to you, perhaps this is a good opportunity to share this section with them . . . because you love them.

If that is something you have said, for shame.

To understand why girls end up with "bad boys" and "good guys" are left confused, we must remember in an earlier section we talked about the difference in how men and women are attracted. Women are attracted on a spectrum.

Men are attracted on a point.

Now, two of the *main* factors in a woman finding a man attractive are 1) his confidence and 2) the interest he shows in her. And therein lies the problem of girls often liking the "bad boys."

See the "good guys" are timid, humble, and rarely assume that an attractive girl is interested in *little ol' them*. Flirting of the female variety is confused for just being kind.

The "bad boys" are arrogant, pretentious, and can't fathom that an attractive girl isn't interested in the *awesomeness that is them*. Even the spurns of an attractive woman are interpreted as unapologetically borderline obsession.

And while slightly annoying, the "bad boys" are, in the end, both persistent and flattering. And if the "bad boys" think so highly of themselves, then women start to think, maybe, just maybe, there is something there they should like too. Not to mention that brash confidence usually plays out in a successful career (albeit an affair or two as well, but that is a couple kids away).

Basically, it's not that women go after "bad boys," but rather that "good guys" won't grow a pair (of eyes to see a great opportunity).

ADVICE THROW DOWN

Ladies . . . you will have to put yourselves out there if you want a "good guy." It may be tough, but it sure is better than just putting out to the "bad boys."

"Good guys" . . . come on man. Just take a leap of faith and realize that in the end, women really want you—but as a man, not a puppy.

"Bad boys" . . . well played. Well played indeed. But don't worry, when you make your money, put on 50 pounds, and are on your third marriage, you'll be calling a "good guy" for life advice.

AN EASY, NONCONFRONTATIONAL WAY TO GET A GIRL'S NUMBER USING FACEBOOK

You meet someone at a party.

She is beautiful and you really want to ask her out.

But maybe the timing isn't right, or you are too nervous or you're not sure if she's dating someone. Whatever the reason, you leave numberless.

But don't worry, because you chatted with her for fifteen minutes and got her first name and college. So after two hours of Facebook stalking, you find her.

You're in luck.

The next day, send her a message like this on Facebook, "You know, I had a great time meeting you and wanted to ask you on a date, but unfortunately, you ran off before I could get your number and now I'm stuck because I would never ask out a woman on Facebook. Do you know anyone that could help me find it?"

If she responds, you're golden, if not, then by the process of deduction, you're one step closer to golden.

Now, don't use this ALL the time; man up and get their number in person too!

Also, remember, if you have not met the woman, do NOT use this tactic. That is just creepy.

TWO STEPS TO ASKING A WOMAN OUT

I'm going to keep this section real simple.

STEP 1: Call her on the phone or talk to her in person one-on-one.

With me still?

STEP 2: Then say, "Can I take you on a date?"

Summary: One-on-one and use the word "date."

Feel free to re-read this section if you have any questions.

A HARSH LETTER TO GUYS FROM GIRLS PLAYING "HARD TO GET"

The following is a letter that my dating blog received one day after a rant about how girls play too hard to get. It helped me to move on quicker from girls in my past, so I thought it wise to add it here. Don't always give up so easily, but know that if it feels too hard, it probably isn't worth it.

Remember: **falling in love isn't work—staying in love is.**

Dear Boys that Think We Are Playing Too Hard to Get,

We really just aren't interested.

And we don't have to go through some elaborate scheme to try and attract you. Truth is we are just more attractive to you because we don't want you (and *all* of us are guilty for wanting what we can't have).

If you ask us out and we are interested, we are going to say yes. It's simple. Some girls are psychologically insane and do the opposite, but hey, that's not the type of person you want anyway (the type with self-destructive tendencies).

"Hard to Get" is not real. It's a made up fairy tale so you can believe that you're somewhat attractive and put yourself in the offense. We're not interested. Sorry. Someone else will be.

Move on.

Truthfully,

Normal Girls

WHAT MEN WANT WOMEN TO KNOW

DON'T BE A PAINE OR A PAIN—NOT *TOO* AVAILABLE

G uys are usually pretty simple creatures.
If they work for something, they like it more than if they don't.

Thomas Paine once penned, "What we obtain too cheap, we esteem too lightly" (*The Writings of Thomas Paine*, edited by Moncure Daniel Conway, New York: G.P. Putnam's Sons, 170, originally in *The American Crisis*).

Paine speaks of things being too easy.

Pain is when things are too hard.

There is a tenuous balancing act that must be performed when being pursued.

I've heard it described as hunters and moose (which I really want to be moosen or moosie or meese . . . but whatever). Guys like to hunt and are fine putting in a lot of work if they know they have the chance to get a kill. They don't mind driving, searching, moose calling, wearing camouflage, or waiting—if they can see the moose tracks and hear the moose calling back.

What gets boring is when the moose is laying on the front porch of the hunting lodge.

So too in dating.

There needs to be a balance struck where you aren't too available, but interested. Don't give them a gun and crawl into the back of the pickup truck, but let them know that it is hunting season.

When you are too forward, guys think that you are desperate and that must mean that other guys aren't interested and that must be because you aren't what they are looking for.

But then again, when you are too distant, guys think that you are stuck up or just not interested.

It can be a super hard balance to strike, but many have, and I have confidence that you can too!

Here's the trick: whenever you want to text them or call them, ask yourself this simple question, "If I were my best friend, what would I tell me to do right now?" It is easy to be objective when it isn't us that we're thinking about. Emotions play such a strong role.

Take a break, think straight, and remember to be a moose somewhere between Paine and pain.

HOW TO GET A GUY TO LIKE YOU

Two simple steps: shorter skirts and lower shirts.

You will get lots of boys to like you . . . stupid, shallow, and worthless guys.

Nothing like what you are looking for.

So let's talk about how you can get a real good guy to like you, even when you're not his typical type.

There have been times in my life where the girl I ended up liking was not my type. And while I have dated many types, there was only one time I dated someone who *wouldn't* be described as "energetic."

This is what happened:

She was cute, but, again, not my type. She was taller, had dark hair, and was super quiet, calm, and chill. I always thought of us as just friends. We hung out in a group together and when I would tell the group about my dates, she would occasionally give advice. That was about our relationship. Then one day the group all left and it was just her and me. Usually, even with great friends, if you are one-on-one with a member of the group for the first time, it can be awkward.

But surprisingly, it was just fun. She was interested in getting to know me better and then opened up when I asked about her. For the first time, I saw a sparkle in her eye that I didn't notice before.

I finally asked her, "Why have we never gone on a date?"

She said, "Because I don't want to be one of those 'Zack Oates girls.'"

While I probably should have at least felt the dig a little . . . being the painfully obtuse optimist that I am, I just didn't hear a "no!"

I said, "What if I promise to only take you on dates that I have never been on with anyone else?" She agreed and out we went. We actually became official too. We ended up breaking up when she got deported, but I was always surprised at how far things went.

In analyzing what she and others in a similar situation did differently, here are the Five Steps to Getting Someone to Like You When You're Just Not Their Type:

- STEP One: Don't be a horrible person. (Do not proceed to Step Two until you un-mean-girls-ify yourself.)
- STEP Two: Find times to spend in groups with your target.
- STEP Three: Show them you are *awesome* without paying extra attention to them or trying too hard.
- STEP Four: Get them alone. (CAVEAT: don't be creepy about this.)
- STEP Five: Show *genuine interest* in them. Ask real questions. Listen. Make eye contact.

So even if, or especially if, you are not their type, it isn't lost; you just need to work a little bit more to win them over. To have a shot, you must first get in their sights. Then, just stay still enough for cupid's arrow to hit the target.

And if this process doesn't work, there are only three reasons why it isn't working: 1) you aren't being blunt enough, 2) you really just aren't their type and should be offended, 3) you went to step two too soon.

FOUR STEPS TO GET A GUY TO ASK *YOU* OUT

Should guys ask girls out?
Yes.
Does the guy that the woman *wants* to ask her out usually ask her out?
No.
[High pitched nasally voice] "I *never* get asked out," they complain. "I'm a victim in this terrible dating game," they whine. "All guys are just dumb," they moan. I say "they" because I know that isn't you. You are the type to do something about it. After all, you made it all the way to this section.

If you are a woman and not getting asked out and want to be getting asked out, you are either

1. Ugly (. . . meaning that you are unkind)
2. Using Tinder wrong
3. Underestimating what it takes to get asked out.

Chances are it is the third.
So, from this guy's perspective, here are four steps to get a guy to ask you out:

STEP ONE: TOUCH HIS ARM

Okay . . . a note to all you "friend zoners" out there, you really need to step outside your comfort zone. Do not treat all boys the same. One of the easiest ways to do this is to grab the back of their arm and hold it for a second or two.

STEP TWO: LAUGH AT HIS JOKES

Every guy thinks he is funny . . . let him. Time will show him that he isn't, but to get asked out, you must play a little bit of this funny game. *But,* beware that you don't laugh at something too hard. That is always awkward. A good benchmark: your face shouldn't hurt at the end of a date. If it is a natural smile, you'll just feel happy, not like you need to ice your cheeks.

STEP THREE: QUESTIONS WITH EYE CONTACT

Asking questions and seeming involved in his answers through eye contact can really seal the deal of showing your interest. None of this head swivel at a party looking for the next conversation garbage.

STEP FOUR: SUGGEST AN ACTIVITY (**THE KEY STEP**)

(Every place and everything in the world is great—I just told you that so you won't be lying when you say this next part.) Think of some obscure thing or a new restaurant or a cool local place and say, "Have you ever heard of _____? Oh man, I heard it was so great! We should totally go there sometime!"

And then your job is done.

If you have touched his arm, laughed at his jokes, asked questions with eye contact, and suggested an activity, and he *has not asked you out*, then . . . good for you. You either know that he isn't interested or you have discovered that he is too dense to realize you're interested—and you don't really want your kids carrying on those stupid genes, do you?

So use these four steps freely and realize that there is no need to complain about not getting asked out; you control who asks you out a lot more than you think.

AN OPEN LETTER TO WOMEN PLAYING TOO HARD TO GET

Dear All Women that Play Too Hard to Get,

Hi. I tried writing this a few times, but wasn't quite sure what to say. I mean, how often do you write a letter to most women on behalf of most guys?

So let me start by saying, wow! Really, you are awesome and beautiful and fun and smart! You really are! You are quite the catch.

Let me continue by saying, ya know what . . . ? We are too.

We know you want some caveman Krull the Warrior King to go out of his cave hunt you down and bring you back victorious, but what you may be forgetting is that we too are looking. We too have other things going on and if you play too hard to get, we will lose interest because some other shiny object will come along. (Let's face it, how far have you seen a dog chase one car?)

Or worse than losing interest . . . we will catch you.

And then, in the clutches of our semi-appropriate spooning position with some romantic comedy playing in the background it will hit us—in all of the chasing, you gave us far too long to romanticize about who you are. Since we never got a chance to open up and have you do the same, we are in love with our perfectly perceived projection of you . . . not really you. And while you might be falling for your Bennybooboopedoo, we, on the other hand, realize that you *are* our cucumber sandwich and we just want poker night.

It is at this moment we start to realize how badly you treated us while we were pursuing. And in the end, somewhere between the credits and the home DVD screen, the decision is made that while we will continue to play your game, this victory will not be carried back to the cave.

So take this advice: if you like us, play nice; if you don't, no dice. Play coy, play intrigue, play genuine . . . but don't play *too* hard.

For yeah, you are a catch; but there are a lot of fish in the sea. And sometimes, when we play your game, it turns into our game of catch and release.

Sincerely,

The Guys You Wish You Were With Ten Years from Now

ZERO TO FIRST DATE

HOW TO TURN DOWN A DATE

*B*efore we get into the mechanics, we need to talk about turning down dates.

Are you obliged to go on a first date with someone who asks? No.

(Period.)

I don't care what other people say, sometimes you just know that there isn't a snowball's chance in hell that things are going to work out. Don't waste your time or money chasing shadows down roads that very obviously go off a cliff.

Now, the same goes for every date after that too.

The key is be kind when you do turn down a date.

Let me set the stage: I had flirted a couple times with this really pretty woman. We bumped into each other every now and then and always had great uplifting banter, but I never got her number. Then at one party we talked for a few hours. As the night wore on, we ended up on the couch talking.

Then sitting close couch talking.

Then cuddling sitting close couch talking.

Then hand rubbing arm cuddling sitting close couch talking.

Things were going well (*right??*). I decided I would go on a (very short) limb and ask her out.

So I turn to her and say, "Can I take you out to dinner this week?" (I know I was supposed to say *"May* I take you out . . ." but I was in the moment and it all happened so quickly.)

She stopped caressing my arm.

It was very silent.

And I kid you not, this is what she says as she is cuddling with me after hours of heavy flirting, "Ummm . . . I'm not too sure about that."

Maybe I mumbled and she didn't understand?

Nope.

She heard just fine.

"Wait," I retorted, "like a dinner date."

"Yeah, I heard you. But no."

All I could say was, "Oh."

I mean, what else was there to say?

That would be a very good example of how *not* to turn down a date.

Realize that no matter who is asking you out, it takes a dose of courage and a slice of humble pie . . . which they do not need shoved in their face. They are putting themselves out there and making themselves vulnerable to you. So give them the respect they deserve.

If you are going to turn them down, be sure to first express sincere gratitude. Not pity. Not like a whole, "awh, aren't you the sweetest thing thinking that a tiny person like you can be with an awesome person like me," but genuine gratitude that they would ask you out.

Then give them a reason. Here is a list of appropriate and inevitable ones they will hear:

1. *It is really bad timing.* They hear: It is really bad timing . . . and the timing is when you are here.
2. *I just started dating someone.* They hear: I just started dating my imaginary friend.
3. *I really need to focus on work/school.* They hear: I really need to focus on curling/watching YouTube videos on ski ballet (a real thing, look it up)/reading a book about dating.

4. *I don't really see us as more than friends.* They hear: I don't really even see us as friends.

It will be hard, but be as honest as your heart will let you while keeping theirs in mind. Make sure that you let them know again how much you appreciate them asking and then end it just how you would kill an injured butterfly—swift, precise, and humane.

ASKING OUT *WILL* GET AWKWARD, AND THAT'S OKAY

Reader beware—there is a little bit of cursing in this story.

I had broken up with a girl a month earlier and was still (pretending to be) upset about it. I had eaten my ice cream, but I still felt a bit salty about dating. I decided I would take a new initiative and ask out my neighbor who was far out of my league. Her name was Michelle (name has not been changed).

She was beautiful, super kind, funny, and a perfect party host. She dressed like a Polo model, cooked like Paula Deen, and either didn't eat her food or worked it all off.

I did my recon and found out she was single. So off to the races.

From previous encounters (stalkings) I knew that she loved to bake and was from the South. So I got a bag of flour, drew a flower on it (see what I did there . . . ?), and brought it over to her apartment to "call on her" (as they say on the hot side of the Mason-Dixon) and ask her out for a date.

I got a pep talk from my roommates, a final call of confirmation from her friend of her single status, and marched over to her apartment to ask her out and, doubtless, have a great story to tell our grandchildren.

Now—no matter how hard we all try, there will always be people who don't like us for one reason or another (or none). Well, unbeknownst to me, the captain of my hater cheer squad happened to be Michelle's roommate. Let's call her . . . Satine (name has been changed . . . but only slightly).

I knocked on the door of my soon-to-be former future ex-girlfriend, Michelle.

The door opened.

My mouth dropped.

"What are *you* doing here?" Satine stood before me, facial expression cutting my heart with degrading daggers of dumbfounded-ness.

"Uh . . . I'm here to see Michelle. . . . Is she here?"

I saw Michelle sitting on the couch and shuffled past Satine to occupy the spot next to her. Satine took a seat across from us on the coffee table and began to burn a hole through my shaken self-confidence.

"Um . . ." I looked at Michelle, hoping to get some reassurance.

None.

Just slight confusion.

My mind was racing. *Okay, Zack. Stick to the plan. The bag—go to the bag!*

"I know you like to bake, so I brought you this flower" [hold up bag and chuckle].

Silence. (A lot of silence.)

". . . Well I was wondering if I could ask you to lunch this week because—"

Satine immediately stood up and clapped her hands. "HEEEEEEEEEEEEEEELLL NO! No no no no *no*! There is no way that you are taking out my roommate, Zack Oates! None. I'm sure you are a nice guy, but no! Michelle, you can make your own decision, I guess." [Exacerbated sigh] "I just . . . I'm leaving. I can't see this. Let me know when he's gone."

And with that, she went to the kitchen, grabbed a small kitten to eat with her side of Oates and went to her bedroom.

Hmm . . . that *wasn't the plan*, monologued my deductive reasoning.

Michelle smiled, politely declined the date, but at least accepted the flour.

An hour later, I got a call from Satine to apologize for her actions. She admitted that she wasn't sure why she hated me so much, but she was sure it was because I had done something to someone she liked at one point but just couldn't remember when or who or what (I didn't argue with her on the specifics). But we did make up and while we have never hung out *on purpose*, we have shared a few smiling hello's and exchanged pleasantries.

And as for Michelle, a couple years later we ended up dating and had a great time, although we both realized it wasn't the right path.

The only reason I share this agonizingly awful story is to show you that asking out can be awkward. Prepare for that inevitability and push through. Anytime you go out on a limb, there is a chance it will break. And after you cower on the ground in pain for a little bit, pick yourself back up, get a running start, and fly.

Just remember, someone rejecting you doesn't say anything about you, it just means that the match isn't good. Like root beer and soy sauce. Both are great, but not together. And that's okay. You'll find your vanilla ice cream or your rice soon enough.

NINE SUGGESTIONS TO A GREAT FIRST DATE

The waiting, the cotton mouth, the anxiety leading up to that door knock for a first date can be painful, at best. There is so much riding on it, and everything up until this point has been to *get* to this point.

Dating is like baking a pie.

All that work: buying, prepping, rolling, and pre-heating. Now, if the oven isn't hot enough, or too hot or you realize that you forgot a key ingredient, you're going dessert-less. But much like pie, there isn't just one right way to do things. So the following are some guidelines to have a sweet and filling first date.

1. PREPARE: If you asked, have a plan. Never ever ever ever ever ever ever . . . ever . . . ask the person what they want to do when they get in the car. It is so incredibly tacky that I can't even write about it anymore.
2. INFORM: If you are doing something that requires a certain type of clothing, inform them. One time when my date planned the activity outside in the winter, I was stuck in the snow with no jacket because I didn't want to man up and tell her I was cold. I ended up taking frequent trips into the bathroom to warm up. Don't say what *specifically* to wear, like stilettoes, but just say generals, like, "We will be going on a hike," or "We'll be on a boat," or "We'll be outdoors in the friggn' cold weather." You get the idea.
3. BE ON TIME: Why would you ever be late to a date? Punctuality shows respect. I have learned from a very sad experience that being late is a terrible idea. Once when I was a candy shop dater, I was late for a date because I was on another. It was a double date and instead of covering for me, the other guy outed me. Smart girl to not go out with me again.
4. DITCH YOUR PHONE: Look . . . just put it away. No need to have a pocket or purse buzzing throughout the date. And ladies, when we get your door and walk around the car, that isn't the time to check your phone. Yeah, we see you Miss Not-So-Sneaky-Pants.
5. MAKE IT SHORT: A great first date should be frozen yogurt or a lunch or a quick dinner and then done. Keep it under two hours—I recommend no more than 90 minutes. The longer it drags on, the less interesting you become. A movie should never be part of a first date. Period.
6. IF YOU ASKED, PAY: If they are spending their time with you, make sure that you pay for them.
7. ASK QUESTIONS: Don't just ask about what their interests are, but figure out why those are their interests. Small talk is fine, but tip-toe into medium chatting on a first date to prepare for your deep conversations that come if all goes well.
8. LISTEN: Stop talking about yourself. Find out about them.
9. BREATHE: Realize that it is a first date. It is okay. Don't stress. Worst case: you can get some free food or at least a good story.

FOUR STEPS TO PICKING A RESTAURANT FOR A DATE

If you didn't know guys, a date, 99 percent of the time, includes some kind of food or at least dessert. If she is sacrificing her time running her business, writing her dissertation or even just watching an episode of *the Bachelorette* to go on a date with you, you should at least feed her.

Now, there are two main approaches: making food and going to eat. This section is going to cater to the latter (see the bonus section for a great cooking date idea).

- STEP One: The day before the date, call her to ask her if she has any allergies or foods she hates.
- STEP Two: Look for two restaurants/dessert shops that fit the allergies and food preference of your date that are within your budget. If you're not sure what your budget is, take a personal finance course. Honestly.
- STEP Three: Choose *two* places that look good to you. For this example, I will choose PF Chang's and California Pizza Kitchen.
- STEP Four: When you pick her up and you are on your way to the area of the date, ask her which *type* of restaurant she would like. For my example, I would say something along the lines of, "I have two choices for a restaurant. Would you prefer Chinese or American food?" Let her choose without telling her the restaurants and then just drive there and surprise her. If she ends up hating that particular place, that's fine because you have your backup.

This works so much better than just taking a girl somewhere without her having any say or even worse . . . the kiss of death, "So . . . where do you want to eat?" I've found that while women might not always know what they want, they know what they do *not* want.

If you ask "Where do you want to eat?" they are likely to respond, "Anywhere . . . I'm fine with whatever!" And the following conversation will ensue.

"Denny's?"

"No . . ."

"Arby's?"

"Good food, better people, but nah."

"Something fancy?"

"Not really my thing."

"PF Chang's?"

"I've only eaten there once and it wasn't amazing."

"So where do you want to go then??"

"Wherever . . . I'm not picky."

Listen, fellas, dating can be a lot better if you just plan ahead. As painful as it may be, a poorly prepared date is much worse for the girl. Follow these four steps to picking the restaurant for a date and you will find your evening full of delicious enjoyment and sweet conversation.

DO NOT ASK FOR A SECOND DATE AT THE END OF A FIRST

Gentlemen, gentlemen, gentlemen . . . [eyebrow rub] . . . [Pause for a slightly condescending glare over the glasses] [Sigh]

How do I put this?

Stop.

Just stop.

You are bold enough to ask her out, smart enough to plan a great date, cordial enough to provide a fun time, calm enough not to do something stupid . . . and then you blow it all at the doorstep. You might as well take off your shirt and show her you have a heart shaved on your chest (which, incidentally, is not a great way of getting a second date #personalexperience).

Open curtain at amateur night:

"I had a great time," he stammers.

"Me too . . . ," she replies.

"Would you like to go on a second date?"

"I . . . uh . . . well . . ."

This is about when Cupid wants to throw a brick at your face. See, there are only five possible scenarios at this moment of a date:

1.   She had a good time and is excited you asked her out.
2.   She had a good time but now you seem too eager and she is questioning if she really had a good time.
3.   She had an okay time and needs a good's night rest to let the date set in before making her decision and now feels undue pressure and that you like her too much and is a little weirded out.
4.   She did not have a good time but awkwardly says yes and is forced to go out with you again.
5.   She did not have a good time and tells you no on the doorstep and you don't go on dates for a couple of weeks and talk about this mean girl who told you no.

If it is a one in five shot of being a good idea, that usually means—*it is not a good idea!*

I put a question out to a few thousand people if it was appropriate to ask out on a second date at the end of the first. While *single women* almost unanimously agreed that this is a terrible idea, there was one group who thought it was completely normal and appropriate: *single men.*

Go figure.

So what do you do? Let's try this again.

Open curtain at a great community theater show:

"I had a great time," he stammers.

"Me too . . . ," she replies.

"We should do it again sometime. [No wait for response] But thanks for the night and good luck with [insert something from conversation to shows he was listening]!"

[Both laugh]

[Night hug]

[Drop the mic and walk away]

Boom.

Be proud of yourself, you just successfully navigated the trickiest waters other than a first kiss—the first "end of date" doorstep scene.

Pat yourself on the back and go hop on Tinder for an ego boost. You deserve it.

It's always appropriate to tell them that you had a good time and would love to do it again, but to set up a second date right there . . . ? Poor form.

FIVE STEPS TO GETTING A SECOND DATE

So if the doorstep ask-out on a first date is a colossal mistake, how *do* you bridge the gap to a second date? Hint: it starts at the first date.

Once you are actually ready to go on a first date with a girl, how do you make sure it is good enough to score a second? How do you not be a player but still play the game?

Here are five steps with a first date to ensure a second:

- STEP One: Ask her on a first date. #mindblown Remember, use the word "date," give her a time you will pick her up, and pick her up at that time.
- STEP Two: Plan to keep it under two hours. A quick dinner *or* frozen yogurt *or* crepes *or* cupcakes (note there was no "and" there). If they aren't wanting more of you by the end of the date, you gave them too much.
- STEP Three: *Only* talk 20 percent of the time. *This* is the biggest, biggest, biggest mistake guys make. (More on this in the next section.)
- STEP Four: Don't contact her for at least one day. It shows that you aren't too eager and have "stuff" going on, even if it is your fantasy football league.
- STEP Five: Call her to ask her on a second date. Yes, call her. No text, Facebook text, snap, insta, tag, group, LinkedIn, email, pigeon, page, singing telegram . . . okay, maybe a singing telegram, but call her too. Ask her to do something specific in a call under five minutes. For example, "[Small chat] . . . but hey, I wanted to call to see if I can take you to grab a bite to eat and to the [activity] this week!"

If you follow these five steps and she says "No," either she's a troll or you are. If she is, good riddance (thank you, Google for letting me know it isn't "good riddens" . . . that could have been embarrassing if people knew I had no idea how to even pronounce that right, much less spell it #closecall). She would make a terrible mother. If you are a troll . . . well . . . don't know what to tell you, buddy. Shoot lower? But really though, you're fine. Just keep trying—there are green pastures across the bridge of "next time," not underneath it.

WHY GUYS SHOULD TALK ONLY 20 PERCENT OF THE TIME ON A FIRST DATE

Okay . . . so why should you only talk 20 percent of the time?

First, everyone loves talking about themselves, so she will have a great time.

Second, you will appear slightly mysterious.

Third, and most important, the only reason you would want to go on a second date with her is because you like her. Typically, she doesn't ask you on a second date; you ask her. And the only way that you are going to find out if you like her is by learning about her . . . which comes from . . . who knows? Anyone? . . . Bueller?

That's right!

Her talking, not you.

So learn about her on the first date and talk 50-50 for the next two dates. (You will find that you will ease back into that 20 percent thing involuntarily quickly if the relationship progresses.)

So you can charm your way onto a first date, trick a girl to a second date, and maybe even convince a girl to go on a third date . . . but that's when the game ends and you are just left with you. The common misunderstanding is that "the game" is meant to fool someone into falling for you—but it isn't. It is to break down the initial walls to see if love is even there.

PRACTICE SAFE DATING: USE PRO*TEXT*ION AND GIVE THEM A PDT (POST-DATE TEXT)

Let me give you some context to this section (rant). I keep pretty detailed track of dating, but in 2010 I did particularly well at bookkeeping. I went on 159 dates. I spend an average of $30 per date so in total I spent a little over $4,770.

Now, if my dating budget was my post-date texting plan, I would have spent a little under $1,000 *per text*.

That is right, I received five post-date texts in 2010.

Five.

That means that 97 percent of dates did not result in a post-date text. People seemed surprised when I tell them this . . . but never anyone I took out.

I did a small study and found that if someone *sent* a post-date text, there was a 70 percent chance that they wanted to go out again. . . . Yet, if they *didn't* send a post-date text, there was a 60 percent chance they weren't trying to say anything at all—good or bad.

And almost all of those 60 percent would be interested in another date.

Girls . . . seriously, make it easier for us. Again, guys are simple creatures.

If you would like to go out with us again, send the text. If not, then don't.

Guys . . . if a girl takes you out, show her you are grateful.

Oh yeah, and if you don't have text messaging, maybe you should try dating an Amish guy. I hear they're cool with stuff like that.

THE THREE-POINT RULE: KNOW WHEN TO GIVE UP

I always had so much trouble knowing when I was being persistent and when I was being a pest. I wanted to work for a girl, but I never wanted to feel that I was the topic of "ugh, not this guy" roommate conversations.

When I came up with the three-point rule, it made dating and that pursuit phase so much better.

So this is how it breaks down to know when to *stop* trying to pursue.

As you reach out to the person, they get points, as they reach out to you, those points are deducted. If they ever get to three points, you stop. You're done.

Isn't going to happen.

It eventually will . . . but not with them.

Now just as not all cupcakes are equal (from stupid, stale, store-bought to homemade, professional-looking with the cream cheese frosting and filling in the middle still slightly warm from the oven), so too, not all forms of communication are equal.

> **One point**: call, voice mail (if it goes right to VM, it doesn't count as a call), text, social message that you know they received, or email.
> **Two points**: call+voice mail or drop by.
> **Three points**: dropping something off for them.

The goal is to stay at 0.

When they get to three points . . . give up.

Because, Mr. Churchill, with all due respect . . . sometimes you really should.

Now, *rarely* do you meet a four-point person, but they do exist.

Keep your dignity. Keep score . . . *until* you have kissed two consecutive times. Then there is no scoring . . . or I guess then there *is* scoring. Hiooo! #highfive

. . . #lefthanging

HOW TO DATE WHEN YOU HAVE OCD

If you are like me and the kind of person that has straightened picture frames in a gas station fast food joint before, you probably have a little bit of obsessive compulsive disorder.

So what's the problem with this?

In business, in friendships, in family life, in chore duties, in personal hygiene, in problem solving, this is a blessing. You pay attention to details and ascribe meaning to them that will allow you to make split second decisions that typically take lengthy reasoning because, subconsciously, you've already thought it all through.

But, if you are pursuing someone . . . oy vey!

Here is the issue: you think about the potential relationship over and over and over and try to figure out what to say and how to say it and when to call and what to text. Then, when you finally do see the other person, you seem odd and robotic.

So here are five remedies I've discovered that are my proverbial OCD meds:

1. Like other people. Have a few people that you are semi-interested in, but keep your number manageable, as we already talked about.

2. Before calling them, do an act of service. By the end, hopefully, you've forgotten to call/text.

3. Only text them out of the blue one in five times you think about texting them.

4. Set a limit on how many times you can talk to friends about them in a day. I try to make that one or two.

5. Only look at their Facebook pictures once a week. *Even if* a pic of her comes up in your newsfeed with some guy that is *blatantly* less cool than you.

Remember, when you seem unduly weird around your love interest and act drastically differently around them than you do around their roommates, they begin to feel that you either don't like them or like them too much. And even if they do like you, they probably don't feel the same way about you as you do about them, yet. You've been thinking about them twenty times a day—while maybe you were one passing thought to them. Be normal, as much as you have to fight for it, until you give them a *chance* to like you. Because honestly, deep down, you probably aren't in need of medication, just understanding. It's not just about the art, but also the framing.

So give them a good picture of you . . . but just make sure the frame isn't crooked.

DON'T PUT STOCK IN THE MOMENT'S EMOTION

My friend and his fiancé were playing tennis.

They were about two weeks away from getting married and everything was going well.

But something changed on that court.

Maybe she wasn't looking as good, maybe he was a bit sick, maybe things were just off. Whatever the reason, he all of a sudden . . . just didn't feel it.

As a result, he almost broke off the entire thing.

Luckily, he didn't, and 25 years later when he told me the story, he has a very happy and fulfilling marriage.

As he was telling me this story, I couldn't help but think of what that meant for me and dating and how often I put so much stock in my *current* (moment by moment) emotions on a date that I don't give things a chance.

See, if I felt "off" about a date, I didn't ask them out again; if I felt "on," I did.

But *whoa whoa whoa whoa*! There are so many factors that go into how I *feel* at any given moment, only a portion of which have anything to do with the date. My emotions might be completely out of both her control and mine when I arbitrarily decide to take my emotional temperature.

It isn't about that moment as much as it is how things are trending over time.

There are plenty of emotional snapshots, or thin slices, that, when taken for what they are, look "off." In the long run, they are actually "on" and, quite frankly, visa versa.

It is just like stocks. Take a look at these three stocks. Looking at these, would you say they are good or bad investments? (Dollars per share is on the right and time is on the bottom in each chart.)

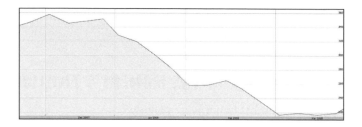

STOCK ONE

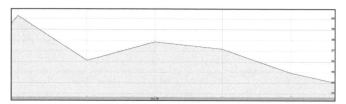

STOCK TWO

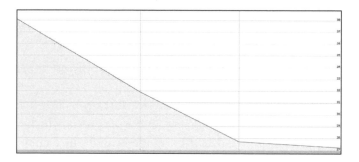

STOCK THREE

They all look pretty bad in these snapshots. Well, do you know who they are? Here is the whole picture, with the portion above noted.

One is actually Google.

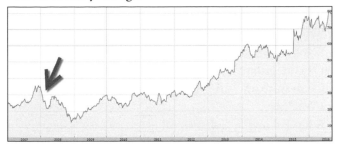

Two is Apple when Steve Jobs died.

And yes, my fellow millennials, three is the opening STINK of our beloved Facebook.

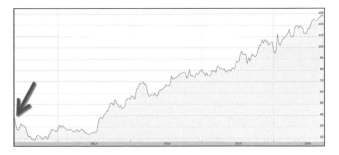

Any stock can have a bad day.

These are all snapshots that make these stocks look like an awful investment, but if you look at the *trends*, these moments are just bad examples of a positive trend.

Conversely, there are stocks like Enron, where it looks like it is heading up with great days and then crashes and dies (much like my third dates).

So what are you expecting me to do, Zack? Go in with a brazen blindfold over my heart and put on my accounting hat to calculate the positive investment potential of a relationship?! No!

What I'm saying is that **we go in with our minds and hearts open to the potential of love while giving the relationship a chance despite an "off" day and not giving *too* much credit to an "on" day.**

What I'm saying is that we all need to do an honest inventory of how much stock we place in our emotions and I, for one, have realized that I've passed a lot of great trends because of a snapshot at the wrong time.

What I'm saying is that we all need to take a step back and not stress so much because it is one moment.

The on or off calibration of human emotions is a highly inaccurate estimate in the moment, for a moment. From what I hear, even marriages have on days and off days, on weeks and off weeks, and yes, even on months and off months.

Because, as my friend proved on that tennis court and as those snapshots of some of the most successful companies in the world metaphorically prove, if there is commitment *and* love, chances are you'll bounce back.

STOP LYING IN DATING . . . BE *YOU*

I had been going out with this girl for a few weeks and we were starting to get a little more serious—becoming more comfortable with each other. One Saturday we went on a pretty casual date to a community theater, hit up the hot tub, and then went off to grab a bite.

By eating time, it was late. We were both tired and hungry.

About fifteen minutes into the dinner I had a sudden rush of fear.

Oh no! She hasn't laughed the entire time I've been sitting here! I'm a terrible date!

And that is when it hit me.

No . . . , I thought. *I'm just comfortable.*

See, I've realized that on so many of my dates, I was lying. And so are you.

We lie when we are going out to a dance party and pretend to have a blast when we really want to be home watching fail videos.

We lie when we open doors for women only for the first few dates.

We lie when we say that we aren't picky about restaurants and then end up only wanting to eat at one place.

We lie when we read intellectually stimulating books just to say that we did.

So let's all just stop.

Stop pretending.

Too many guys have married a chill girl only to find out she was completely crazy and mean.

Too many girls have married a perfect guy only to discover he is a total creeper and abusive.

On the not severe side, too many have dated a really fun person to find out they are super lame: a movie goer who hates movies, a partier who hates parties, a person who is only being what they think the other person wants.

Just be you.

Don't stop trying to be better . . . but be honest.

Because I promise, **you will be loved; but the problem is when people fall in love with what you want them to *think* you are. Let them get to know and fall in love with you . . . as you are.**

Yes, it's okay to be tired and hungry and *not* funny. It's okay to have a bad day. It's okay to even be a little vulnerable.

You aren't on some stage trying to entertain your date with a character portrayal of everything they want—*you are sitting at dinner with someone who just wants to be with you.*

So let's try to improve ourselves, but let's be honest with who we are because there is no role in the act of love for liars.

THE LAW OF DIMINISHING DEAL BREAKERS: BE YOU . . . BUT IN DOSES

To help you navigate this awkward balance of being you, but putting your best foot forward, I present the chart explaining The Law of Diminishing Deal Breakers.

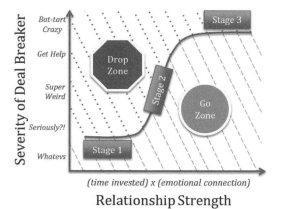

Relationship Strength

The law states that the correlation between the relationship strength and the severity of the deal breaker is a Gompertz function, also known as an "S-curve" (thanks, Internet), where the further you progress in the relationship, the greater the concern must be in order to become a legitimate "deal breaker."

"Relationship Strength" is defined by the time invested multiplied by the emotional connection. It isn't just about connection or time, but both!

Anything that falls into the "Drop Zone" is out like a fat kid in dodge ball.

Everything in the "Go Zone" is on like Donkey Kong.

The severity of the deal breaker is a subjective parameter by the evaluating party.

Let's understand this from the perspective of being observed.

STAGE ONE: FEELING IT OUT

On a first date I wouldn't mention the fact that I have leopard sheets, hot tamale PJ's, bear claw slippers, and a little mermaid pillow case. That's a little too much into the "Seriously?!" boundary.

So keep it normal at the start—even (especially) if you aren't.

Now this does not mean to lie or be brutal. If you don't like parties, you don't have to say, "I hate parties and everyone that goes to them because they are stupid!" You can say, "I would rather do something else next time if that is okay."

Think of this as the "paper bag at a grocery store" stage. You don't want to put too much heavy stuff in here.

STAGE TWO: FEELING GOOD

Here you can begin to explore a little bit of letting them get to know your quirks. Your weird "driving alone in the car" singing habits may be a little too soon here, but start to test the waters with the number of shoes you have, your disdain for open cupboard doors, and your fetish with pulling out nose hairs.

This is the "paper and plastic, please" stage where you can handle a couple jugs of milk or ten frozen pizzas.

STAGE THREE: FEELING SURE

Regardless of how strong your relationship is, everyone has a limit of what they are willing to handle. Things like killing people, *super* [censored] Internet habits or sneezing into your hand instead of your elbow would fall into this category.

This is the "box it up" stage where you move in your baggage.

Moral of this graph: My mother always tells me, "Zack, don't not be you . . . just be . . . *less* of you at first."

LAW OF DIMINISHING DEAL BREAKERS: DOUBT THE BENEFIT

Now this chart isn't just about you giving a slow reveal of your oddness, it can also help you understand your feelings for someone you date.

Before I understood this chart, I asked this girl out. She was beautiful, fun and seemed to be pretty cool. *Then* she revealed that she hates hot tubs.

. . . on a first date.

"WHAT?! HOW CAN YOU POSSIBLY HATE HOT TUBS?!"

I told her, "It goes 1. Religion, 2. Family, 3. Hot tubs." She disagreed.

I never asked her out again.

To me, that fell above the line and entered the "Drop Zone" during "Stage 1: Feeling it Out." I felt like she was putting kitchen knives and bowling balls in that poor paper bag—it just wasn't going to hold.

But in retrospect, I was ridiculous! To stop going out someone because they hate hot tubs? #facepalm

It is one thing to dislike something that I like, but the big question is *why*. See, not liking hot tubs falls into the "Seriously?!" category (for me), which, if I would have invested a little more time or discovered a little more emotional connection, would not have been a deal breaker at all. I would have progressed to "Stage Two: Feeling Good" and it would then be below the deal breaker line.

The process of falling in love with someone is simply understanding them.

That understanding doesn't come through knowing *what* they do/don't do or like/don't like, but though a deeper appreciation of *why* they do/don't do or like/don't like.

Take the hot tub hater, for example. People understand and love her deeply. She has best friends, siblings, parents, (now her husband, who is "Stage Three: Feeling Sure") and yeah, especially God, who thinks that she is a totally incredible person.

And I didn't get a chance to see why they think that because of a "heated" debate. I was too immature to look beyond the curve into "Stage Two" where I could have seen her for the amazing person she is.

Shame on me!

We often get so caught up in the deal breakers that we forget one important fact: once the relationship strength increases, our concern often won't even be a deal breaker—hence, the Law of *Diminishing* Deal Breakers. The further you progress, the less things will throw you off.

Have a few nonnegotiables, and then it all comes down to what was said in an earlier section: **give a person the benefit of the doubt—until they give you reason enough to doubt the benefit.**

And this goes well beyond dating, keep in mind. This is about humanity.

Next time you look at an old person, realize that one time they were held as a baby. When you see the quiet person, remember that they have made people laugh until they cried. As you meet others, assume they are trying to be good.

For in the end . . . don't we hope that others will assume the same for us?

IF I WERE RICH, I'D HAVE BEEN MARRIED YEARS AGO

A few years ago I had a startup. It got some good publicity, I was working with some huge companies and it was a lot of fun.

Then I found out that my main competitor sold for 80 million dollars to Facebook. Ugh. While things turned out fine with my company, it never was sold for that many zeros.

I have, from time to time, imagined what my life would have been like had my company been the one to sell for 80 million dollars. One thing is almost for sure: I'd have been married much sooner.

. . . but not for the reason you think.

I wouldn't be married because I would have found some gold digger, but rather because more girls would have given me a chance.

See, I know that there are people whom I could have married (granted, I'm *so grateful* I didn't so that I could meet my wife), but they just never gave things a shot when I was in the right place.

While money wouldn't have bought them, it might have helped them to go on one more date, keep their mind open a little bit more, ignore some of the stories and preconceived notions of what a dating blogger might be like. We might have fallen in love and gotten married. But it wasn't until Annie that the right girl gave it the right shot at the right time . . . and while I still don't have 80 million dollars, I feel rich (#awwwh).

Now here is where it comes down to what is important: *you*!

All I'm saying is this: there are people, whom you probably already know, that you can marry, if you just give it a shot. Pretend they do have all the money you could ever want and ask yourself if you would honestly try just one more time. Or said another way, pretend you lived in a remote village in China with no Internet and ask yourself if things might work out. It doesn't mean they are the one, but rather they might be one of the ones if you look at things in a different light.

So look over your friend list, overlook your initial impressions, and really look it over. Keep your heart open to the possibility and just give it one more honest chance to find love. I'm not saying find some crazy person and try to fall in love, but don't be so scared because someone isn't as attractive, isn't as funny, isn't as dynamic, or isn't as rich. You may just be seeing things wrong. Because they might not be a millionaire . . . but, I think it was in the Bible or Gandhi or something who penned the ever-true words, "Money can't buy me love."

RELATIONSHIPS

THREE-STEP FORMULA TO CHOOSE YOUR LOVE

"C hoose your love and love your choice" (Thomas S. Monson, "Hallmarks of a Happy Home," *Ensign*, November 1988).

The first time I heard this statement, I felt I understood it. I still think that I get the second part—love your choice. To me, that means being committed.

But what does that first part mean? How do we choose our love?

We often get so lost in a misunderstanding of what it means to choose our love that we never obtain what we want (or at least want to want): marriage. Or better put, a great marriage.

For years I was convinced that I was doing my part to get married, until I realized months before I got engaged that there was a three-word formula. It is a formula for helping us all choose our love—not just waiting around for him or her to appear.

Openness.

Service.

Time.

When I was in school, I met this girl. She was pretty, smart, and motivated, but we weren't really one another's type. I thought she was a little too high-strung, and I could tell she thought I was immature (turns out one of us was right—her). I never asked her out, but we became good friends. Then one day, I thought to put the "choose your love" counsel to the test and see if I could really like her. So I decided I would make myself vulnerable and not even care if she didn't like me back. Every time I saw her, I would give her a compliment, try to make her day a little better, and be more eager to help her out—basically, I served her. Not in a creepy way, but in a way to help her day be a little bit better.

Over time, something happened.

Week One: I did not feel much of a change.

Week Two: I started to notice myself glancing at her more often.

Week Three: I caught myself thinking about her randomly.

Week Four: I noticed butterflies when she came around.

Week Five: I was looking forward to seeing her.

Week Six: I really liked her . . . a lot.

A religious leader who had a long and amazing marriage said, "If every husband and every wife would constantly do whatever might be possible to ensure the comfort and happiness of his or her companion, there would be very little, if any, divorce" (Gordon B. Hinckley, "The Women in Our Lives," *Ensign*, November 2004). By the same token, if singles follow that advice, there would be many more fulfilling relationships.

I finally decided to give myself a chance to fall in love by being open to the possibility of love, serving, and doing it over time.

Openness.

Service.

Time.

That is how you fall in love.

That is how you stay in love.

Sure, she might not have ended up feeling the same way about me, but at least I discovered that we have the power to choose.

It is just like farming.

Plant it (be open), water it (serve), and look after it (give it time). And if it is a good seed, you are giving it a chance to grow. The more we serve someone, the more we love that person. Why do you think Christ loves us unconditionally forever? We fall in love by serving imperfectly for a few hours a week, yet He served us perfectly for our entire lives. What love He must have for each of us!

If you want to love someone, you *might* try this "choose your love" formula out.

If you have lost a little bit of the fire and want to kindle that flame back up, you *must* try this out.

Love is one of the most important things in life, and I, for one, am done waiting for fickle-footed fate to drag me to it. It's my choice.

Now if only there were a formula for getting someone to try this out on us . . .

DTRS

It had been a hot summer day in the backcountry of Utah. I was on a hike with a bunch of my single friends and it was starting to get late. At the turn-around point of this gradual up-hill hike, there was a dried up riverbed at the bottom of a cliff that tickled my curiosity. To get there, I would need to climb down the rock face without the assistance of ropes; but it looked like it would be a blast of a trail run.

I looked at my watch.

Six p.m.

I estimated the jog back to camp would take maybe an hour.

I thought it would be fine and it looked more exciting than going back to where I started, so after a short argument from my friends about the unknown and safety and blah blah blah, I took off.

It would be another six hours before I would see them again.

The night came quicker than expected. Without a moon or flashlight, I was in the pitch black trying to climb up and down 20-foot cliffs, walk on a narrow trail with steep drop-offs on both sides, and wade through cesspools of unknown depths. After hours, I finally found some footprints that I thought would lead me back to the trail and a wash of relief rushed over me . . . but alas, they were mine. I was completely lost in a desert, no doubt filled with animals waiting to prey on a stupid hiker.

Using some very technical Boy Scout survival techniques (yelling), I eventually found my friends on an abandoned road looking for me.

That story is a lot like dating.

Except you're never found and die alone.

Okay, kidding. Kidding!

Let's set the stage with you and an interest of yours.

You've gone on a few dates.

Things are going well.

You've even kissed a couple of times.

So . . . now what?

You are at a turning point where you can go back with your single friends to camp, or take the plunge into the dried up riverbed of the unknown.

You need to DTR.

While it may destroy the relationship, it actually stands for Determine The Relationship.

This is a talk that needs to be handled with care and proper timing.

One of the easiest ways I've found to initiate this conversation is to say something along the lines of, "I really enjoy being with you."

Evaluate their response.

"I don't want to date anyone else."

Evaluate their response.

"So, can I introduce you as my boy/girlfriend?"

Evaluate their response.

If at any evaluation point it looks like the proverbial darkness of night will set in faster than expected, feel free to turn around. But don't be afraid!

Because the worst that can happen is you get lost for a little bit.

But in the end, no matter how dark the night and how awkward the things you had to do (that your publisher won't let you put in this book) are . . . you'll make it out alive and your single friends will be there looking for you on that lonely road back to camp.

So go forth and don't fear the DTR—embrace it, for one day, at the end of that dried up riverbed you'll find something worth the risk to get there.

GIVE THEM THE GIFT OF MISSING YOU

I used to dream about candy cigarettes. I loved them so much. I would go into every candy store I could find to see if they had them.

They rarely did . . . because ya know, it isn't the 1930s, turns out.

But when they did, I would get so excited that I would pay as much as four dollars for a pack (it was in NYC and when I saw the price, I snarkily asked the guy working there if he knew they weren't *real* cigarettes. He asked me to leave). Anyway, a few years ago, I got onto a website and found them for $20 per box that had 36 packs!

I was stoked. I ordered three boxes—108 packs. I put them in my office and ate fifteen packs in three days . . . and haven't touched them since.

There they sit. In my office. Daily I look at them; but never partake . . .

So it is with dating.

Here is the thing that people forget. It isn't about playing the game, but it is about helping the other party realize that you should be important to them. In any relationship, there will be an unbalance of "liking-you"ness until eventually . . . things even out or fizzle out.

But remember the person you are dating only knows two kinds of life: life with you and life before you.

Give them the gift—

The gift of missing you.

Give them a third option of life with you but without you around.

It gives them a chance to really appreciate you. As the actor Al Pacino, in his graceful eloquence of silver-screened wisdom, said, "You know, when you get old, in life, things get taken from you. I mean . . . that's . . . that's . . . that's part of life. But, you only learn that when you start losing stuff" ("Inches" speech during *Any Given Sunday,* 1999).

So be sure to give them a taste of what it would be like *if* they were to lose you. Give them that third option.

Don't take this too far and go dumping that someone you just started dating, but there are things you can do at any stage in a relationship.

If you are married, take a trip with just your friends.

If you are dating, take a night to yourself.

If you are not yet dating, be sure to go out with other people still. Just be cool, man.

If you just met them, give them space.

Don't be so available that you become the proverbial pack of candy cigarettes unattractively begging daily for attention (even if you are a middle child like me). For if the relationship will go well, your naggy-nancy-neurosis will be far less effective than your sweet (albeit chalky) personality.

Simply put: fellas, chill out; ladies, don't be crazy.

PEPTO-BISMOL YOUR RELATIONSHIP

I was about twelve years old when one night, I woke up sick. Super sick.

Like the feeling you get when there are evil elves gnawing at your innards and trying to axe their way out . . . I'm sure you know what I mean.

To my fragile mind, I was certain this was going to be the end of me.

I crawled into my parents' room with my last confession and my final good-byes. My father rolled out of bed and brought me to the toilet where he handed me a capful of Pepto-Bismol.

I refused to take it.

I told him I was too sick.

"Tell Mother I went down bravely."

"Zack," he said with the tired sigh of a patient parent needing to go to work in a few hours, "just take it. Look, it will either make you throw up and you'll feel better, or it will make you feel better and then, well, you'll feel better."

Even at death's doorstep, the logic was sound.

I partook of the bubble-gum elixir and slowly, calmly drifted back to sleep on the cool tile floor. I awoke the next day with a black tongue feeling just fine (seriously, if you take the pink stuff at night and don't wash your mouth after, your tongue will turn black by morning . . . look it up).

Such it is with relationships.

Should you take them to a family dinner?

Should you invite them to the class reunion?

Should you take that next big leap?

I say, yeah!

Look, it is either going to work out or not. If you are to the point that you are thinking about taking that dried up riverbed stroll, then take that next step.

The best Pepto-Bismol for a relationship?

A road trip.

There have been more breakups and fix-downs (the opposite of a breakup?) from road trips than from any other event I can think of. Just pick a place and go there. You may need to turn around halfway, but then again, you may need to take more time off of work.

Because if it isn't going to work out, you'll find out quickly.

If it will, you'll feel better knowing sooner.

Plug your nose, close your eyes, and bottoms up, baby! It's going to be a fun ride.

HOW TO DECIDE BETWEEN DATING TWO PEOPLE

We've all been in the situation where we meet two people pretty close together and we start to like both.

What to do?

To start, we need to lay the groundwork assumption, which I hold to be true; you can only give your heart to one person at a time, and that is a decision you make. You can be kissing multiple people at the same time (which I will *always* and under *any* situation say is a huge *no-no*), but your heart will remain with one person.

But if you are in the process of deciding, what should you do? Sometimes it can be a deadlock.

One is smarter, the other is funnier. One is a little prettier, the other is a little better at social situations. One is more passionate, the other has more direction. One is secure, the other is adventurous. One is really nice, the other is spunky. One you know likes you, the other you hope does.

Keep it simple. Don't just look at how you feel about that person, but look at how you feel about *yourself*.

Don't worry about choosing the hotter one or the better kisser or the one with the better resume or cooler friends, because in the end, when all of that melts away, it exposes the core of any relationship: how you feel about yourself when you are around *and not around* that person, because their influence should go beyond just being in their presence.

But beware!

A dear friend of mine who had two men trying to marry her once told me, "*Do not* wait too long to decide. It will damage the relationship with whomever you choose and you will die lonely surrounded by cats." (I took some liberties with the end of this quote, but it was more of less the gist of it.)

Who inspires you? Makes you feel like a better person? Who doesn't make you feel like some puppet or accessory? That is the seed of a great relationship. And if you put yourself into it and it is right, love will come.

For love is a magic potion that is concocted in the kitchen of decision with a little bit of help from the laboratory of luck.

Oh, and as for my friend? She waited too long to decide and is still single. #feastorfamine

USE YOUR BRAIN *AND* YOUR HEART

It feels so right, but doesn't make sense (heart, no brain) . . . and somehow we move forward.

It makes perfect sense, but doesn't feel right (brain, no heart) . . . and somehow we walk away.

Why?!

Why can't it just all work out?!

Well because the heart and the brain are two very different parts of the love machine.

The brain directs as the steering wheel. The heart moves as the gas pedal.

I have met these girls that were just hot messes. Nothing made sense; but we just had that chemistry. My heart was in it. And I went forward. The brain tried to catch up and try to make sense of things as I fumbled my way around a relationship with them.

When your heart is in it, your brain just has to just figure it out.

I have also met girls that were just perfect. Their families and I got along great, they wanted to save the world, they were independently wealthy, models, spiritual—I mean the only red flag was that they were interested in me. *But,* there just wasn't that spark. My brain was pointing me in the right direction, but I was moving as fast as a junkyard brick.

When your brain is driving solo, your heart is out to lunch with the keys.

It really is that frustrating. It really is that simple.

Love is that mercurial mystery that builds the bridge between the largest chasm known to humankind: the twelve-inch gap between the brain and the heart.

When the heart and mind line up, so do the stars—navigating you to a lovely place.

That's not to say that we aren't at Cupid's mercy and fate's justice when it comes to love. As we talked about, love is a choice. The choice isn't with whom you will fall in love or when, but it is about getting into the car and being open to the open road. We allow the possibility of a final destination enter into our minds and permeate our hearts. Then we move forward.

So be patient. I believe there will come a time when it will happen—that day where your car will be pointed in the right direction with the pedal to the medal. Just don't crash (lose hope) before you get there!

THE FIVE BUCKETS
OF ATTRACTION

FIVE BUCKETS OF ATTRACTION AND HOW TO USE THEM

We each have five buckets of attraction:

1. Physical
2. Intellectual
3. Emotional
4. Spiritual
5. Sexual

Now I know what you're thinking. "Zack, aren't physical and sexual attraction the same thing?"

Well, to be short, no.

Physical is how you think a person looks, sexual attraction is that certain special something that draws you to them. But more on that soon.

Every person has these five buckets of attraction. Each of us has a different level that each bucket needs to be filled and every relationship will fill each bucket different amounts.

Then, on top of everything else, there is the law of timing that glues everything together.

But there is hope, even if your relationship isn't filling all five of your buckets right now. Just figure out which bucket isn't quite filled to your level and then plan dates that will help you to see if the relationship has the potential to fill that bucket to your required level.

So let's dive into these buckets.

BUCKET ONE: PHYSICAL ATTRACTION

A silent rumble of whispers washes across the crowded room as the apartment door closes, admitting a new attendee. Between the over-gelled hair and the under-developed makeup skills, you see a beam of radiance. You are astounded. You want to go up and speak with her . . . but your legs don't have the strength, your stomach doesn't have the nerve, and for the first time in your life . . . you can't think of something to say.

Don't worry . . . it's not love, it is physical attraction.

Happens to the best of us—and to the rest of us—seeing a person across the room who is just simply, in one word, beautiful. I had a lot of trouble with this type of attraction because this is what, more than anything else, gave me sweaty hands. I couldn't think of stuff to say and then because of this . . . no other attraction could develop.

That being said, in dating, you don't have to find a person who makes you fall off your seat, just someone with whom there is physical attraction to some level. Or even someone with whom there could be a potential.

Two quick illustrative stories:

1. I liked a girl. She was okay looking. We started talking . . . I totally fell for her. We dated.
2. I liked a girl. She was extremely attractive at first glance. We started talking . . . suddenly I couldn't have been less attracted to elastic above-the-ankle hipster pants.

Physical attraction, while it may be the most noticeable type of attraction at first, is, in my opinion, the most fickle. It can change in a day based off of a stupid comment or a soul-bearing conversation.

Final word: Keep an eye on your physical attraction level readings. It is a great benchmark for the other types of attraction.

BUCKET TWO: INTELLECTUAL ATTRACTION

"Wait . . . what does that mean again?"

It was the third time I used the word "facetious" that night. Things were not going well.

She had admitted to disliking books, hating documentaries, and finding all museums boring.

It's not that I'm super smart or anything (I mean, I did use the word "facetious" three times in one night. *Synonyms anyone?*), but there was just no intellectual curiosity.

Now I know that sounds harsh, but to be fair, I can think of plenty times where the girl has thought I was an idiot—that's no fun either. It is important that there is an attractive connectedness on a *similar* intellectual plane.

One of my best dating relationships was completely intellectually satisfying. She would speak for about five minutes, then I would return with my retort; then she would have a swift rebuttal and I would shoot back. Her thoughts rolled off her lips and caressed my deepest intrigue. It was a romantic waltz of words that effortlessly danced across hours (eventually though, I decided I wanted a relationship, not a debate partner).

Final word: Don't marry an idiot (unless there is money involved . . . then take your chances) because, while hotness is only skin deep, stupid lasts forever.

BUCKET THREE: EMOTIONAL ATTRACTION

It was our fourth date. I had been playing things off casually and having a great time. Then things took a turn south when she asked the question, "Why do you like [that]?" (I don't even remember what she was talking about; I just remember that penetrating word "why.")

It was weird. I usually don't have a problem talking about my emotions or, quite frankly, myself (in case you haven't figured that out), but I just didn't want to talk to *her* about me, outside of lawn croquet and s'mores. I didn't even want to talk about me not wanting to talk about it.

Soon I realized it must end. But there was a problem . . . I didn't want to talk about it.

So I did what any self-respecting young man would do, I searched for a "deal breaker" in her book and tried to play it up. Unfortunately, she loved Christmas. For one week, I nonstop talked about how much I hate Christmas. (Now I really don't hate Christmas, I just hate decorating for Christmas.) Anyway, she dumped me, I never had to talk about it, and we got on our very merry way. (Yeah, you're reading *that* guy's book on dating. But in my defense, that was when I learned I needed to document my mistakes and figure out how to do things right.)

Emotional attraction is not that you *can't* talk about certain things because of the stupidity of the other person, but that you just never *want* to because of a plethora of possible problems. But if you cannot open up to someone to tell them how you are really feeling, then things will never *ever* work for real.

And can you be you . . . or are you just trying to be who they want you to be? There is a fine line between "expanding your horizons" and faking it. People hate liars. As we talked about, if you are lying in dating, eventually you will hate yourself too.

And how do your life philosophies match up? I dated a girl who wanted to live in the same town as her family for the rest of her life. I liked her and her family, but not *that* much . . . on either account.

Final word: If you have tried to open up about your feelings with your significant other and just can't do it—maybe you need to find another in whom to place significance.

BUCKET FOUR: SPIRITUAL ATTRACTION

I met this girl a few months earlier. We had never even been on a date. We happened to be at the same party and when things were starting to die down I asked, "Do you want to go outside?"

The warm summer breeze kissed our cheeks as we snuggled up close under a blanket, pretending to be cold. We laid there for five minutes without even speaking—just gazing. We started to talk about religion and God and the purpose of life. We chatted for about an hour. I kissed her on the forehead and we headed inside to play the Wii. (I beat her and didn't even feel bad.)

That was it.

No awful ending to this story. We never dated but had a great respect one for another from then on.

Sometimes that happens—even with me, believe it or not.

With very *very* few relationships, I have been able to transition from having fun to talking about spirituality back to fun. But those, ah, those, my dear friends, are the relationships that we must treasure. They are precious gems amidst the rocky road of regretful relationship blunders.

Now if you don't have a spiritual side, get one. And not even because you want to believe in a higher power—but just because relationships are *so* much better with that additional benefit of spirituality. Spiritual-less couples are experiencing a four-sided pentagonal relationship.

As the poet penned, "Be at peace with God, whatever you conceive Him to be" (Max Ehrmann, *The Desiderata of Happiness* [New York: 1995], 10).

But it is not just about both people being spiritual, it is about the mutual attraction—it is about the spiritualties, so to speak, matching up.

I once liked this girl who was a witch. Like an actual witch, not a fill-in for another similar-sounding word. I bought some books to read up on it . . . but the spiritual attraction ended when the weird black magic started (okay . . . it really ended at the "witch" part in general . . . but I did buy a book and read it).

Final word: If you can't get spiritual under the stars (without getting physical), then you need to get out!

BUCKET FIVE: SEXUAL ATTRACTION

PART ONE

We had been hanging out for a few weeks. I was thinking things were going somewhere because everything lined up.

I mean she was attractive, intellectual, emotionally open, and spiritual—it seemed like she was perfect. I took her under the stars, put on the great-date-show and was ready to pull the big move: hold her hand (that has a bit of sarcastic over-tone, in case you didn't catch it).

I started with the classic hand massage and then moved into the interdigitation hand holding with the thumb thing (but just enough of the thumb moving, not so much where you get uncomfortable and none of that arm rubbing junk. Man, I hate it when they rub my arm! Let my hairy arms be, would ya?! Anyway, I digress).

Everything was perfect . . . except for one thing: I felt like I was holding my sister's hand.

It was so awkward.

Our hands wouldn't quite fit, there was a rock right under my back, I didn't want to look at her, and I felt nothing. I mean nothing. I didn't even want to kiss her. In a horrific moment of self-reflective honesty, I realized the facade of four attractions would not support a relationship.

There needed to be that something more, that "x" factor . . . that sexual attraction. (Note to reader: the "x" factor should not to be confused with the "ex" factor, which is kissing a former gf/bf . . . in the tried and tested opinion of the author, *not* recommended.)

I can think a girl is the most beautiful girl in the world—but still not want to kiss her or hold her hand or anything. And I'll be honest in saying that girls will tell me that they like me, but just not in "*that*" way, as they describe it. There needs to be that desire.

One girl told me I was like a "wet keg of gunpowder" . . . meaning all of the potential, but none of the spark. I am still a little burned from that one (not really . . . but I had to throw in the pun).

That measure of carnal desire I define as sexual attraction. It has to be there. It doesn't have to be first on the list, but has to be there . . . in modest amounts. A great relationship can be overrun by this type of attraction, but when used properly, sexual attraction can be the test that proves that all the other attractions really are valid and will heighten them to a new level. (This is one of the reasons I truly believe in no sex before marriage).

And for those that say you have to have sex to see if you are intimately compatible, I totally disagree. I remember one of the best first kisses I ever had. When our lips touched, it was magical. I mean Epcot Center on the Fourth of July couldn't hold a candle to the fireworks that were going off. (Didn't even use tongue.)

On the other hand, a relationship that is built solely on sexual attraction is like trying to balance a tray of red wine-filled stemware over a white carpet on the sharp side of a thumbtack . . . it will fall. It will get messy.

Final word: If she doesn't make you go "WHOPEEE," then you've got an "*oopsy.*"

PART TWO—WAIT FOR SEX

We interrupt this section to bring you an important PSA.

Let's talk about sex . . . and not having it . . . until you should. Glad we had this chat. Now go clean your room.

. . .

Okay but really, I am going to talk about sex (and how most of what I have learned before marriage was taught in fourth-grade health class and bachelor parties).

Right before I got married, I made a comment about being a virgin and apparently many people feel that a never-been-married 29-year-old guy shouldn't be. Well I am here to tell you that you don't need sex to live a fulfilling and happy life. I made a personal choice to wait to have any sexual activity until after marriage and while I'm not judging others who have made different choices, let me tell you why I stuck to my guns. Disagree, you may (Yoda imagery during sex talk . . . that cools the mood), but at least hear me out.

I think sex is special. So special, in fact, that I don't believe that sex should be had outside of marriage.

Many of my friends tell me I'm crazy. "You can't buy a car without a test drive. You can't know if there is chemistry without sex! Do you want bad sex for the rest of your life?" But I'm not buying a car, I'm looking for a spouse. It is like saying, "You don't want going to the moon to be bad."

Let me clarify.

Scenario: I'm going to the moon. I've never been. I'm pretty sure whatever it is going to be pretty cool. So chill your overactive hormonal jet packs. If it is the only moon I've ever been to, it *will* be the best.

Now, as for the chemistry. Let me ask you non-virgins out there . . . have you ever kissed someone before having sex with them? Have you ever held someone's hand before kissing them before having sex with them? Yes on both accounts?

My questioning progresses to a conclusion.

Have you ever held someone's hand and felt a spark?

Kissed them and felt a spark?

Had sex with them . . . and *not* felt that same spark? that chemistry? that je ne sais pas quoi (as they say in America)?

No! The answer has always been, is, and will always be no.

Now they go telling me about this "it physically needs to work" stuff and all . . . but what it really comes down to is chemistry, or sexual attraction.

So, a reason that sex before marriage is not needed (as a perfectly sane choice) is chemistry can be deduced through other ways, such as kissing or even holding hands.

That being said . . . I do *not* feel that people who think differently or had sex before are bad, but rather I am tired of being labeled as "ignorant" simply for following a deeply personal decision.

I know the moon is there. I eventually got there. But I am grateful to share that whole celestial sphere with one person.

THE LAW OF TIMING

A few years ago, I went out with a celebrity blogger. I was nervous—I even washed my car for the date. I would have gotten a wax too . . . but the salon was booked (kidding).

We made dinner, laughed, danced in the kitchen, chatted on the couch, and just had an overall fun time. No detail spared, every dollar that should have been spent was.

I'm golden, I thought.

After some back and forth texting over the next couple of days, I finally ask her if I would be able to see her again. I pulled out the text card because it wasn't super official, but she knew I would want to see her again.

Money.

Everything was there to have the relationship start to rise.

. . . but sometimes it isn't about the ingredients.

Her text back started off with two words, "Yeah, sure . . ."

Like that feeling when you used starch instead of flour; I had a sinking feeling in my gut. I almost didn't want to keep reading.

The text continued ". . . but know that it won't be romantically."

Fool's gold.

You see, a few days before our date, I called her to change our date from Friday to Saturday. After all, *what could happen in a day?*

Great question. Let me answer that.

She had a guy friend call her whom she had known for years, they went out last minute and hit it off. By Sunday they were officially on and I was officially off.

Burnt.

That's what happens when you are 24 hours too late.

Timing isn't always a thing, but when it is, it is *the* thing.

That's why you shouldn't leave the house with cupcakes in the oven, or you may come home to find out that someone already frosted and ate them for you.

The law to which all buckets of attraction bow is the timing. If the attraction and willingness just miss each other by a year, a week, or by ten minutes, it won't work. There has to be five buckets of attraction filled to the required level for you and five for them. A total of ten.

Nine out of ten doesn't cut it.

There is nothing you can do about it if one of the parties is not ready or one of your buckets is unfilled. If you want to build a solid relationship, you both have to be ready to rock at the same time.

But it's important to note: don't hate yourself for not loving the perfect guy or girl. People say, "When it's right, it's right" (It is that "when" word that kills single people). But I look at it this way, if everyone saying this has found love, 60 million Frenchmen can't be wrong.

You deserve someone who is ready for sometwo.

Final word: Sometimes you're not a day late, just a dollar short. And if you're on tick when she's on tock, your hope to click is out of luck.

WAIT BEFORE YOU BREAK

TEN OF THE WORST *REAL* REASONS PEOPLE HAVE DUMPED OTHERS

I don't feel this section needs a lot of commentary other than this: don't. So here are the top ten worst reasons to break up from friends of mine.

10. The ol' "it's not me, it's you not being perfect enough" routine.

Chelci related, "You're an amazing person, have so many great qualities and I really do care about you but I'm waiting on the 'perfect' girl."

9. "You're too smart/dumb . . ."

Mark said, " 'You're too smart for me.' She was right."

8. ". . . and so am I."

Julia said, "One time a two weeker told me he didn't think we were intellectually compatible. I told him I knew what that meant and I was pretty sure he wasn't calling me smart. . . .

"2 hours later he came back to me and apologized and wanted to get back together, which was not the mutually agreed upon outcome."

7. "God told me . . . or like He's telling me . . . right now"

Kaitlin shared, "My friend was broken up with unexpectedly via a PRAYER."

6. "Pickings are too slim"

Elizabeth related, "'You're too fat for me.' I was 110 at 5'8" and the girl he was cheating on me with was 60 pounds heavier than me."

5. This one is pretty legit, but still I can't believe that guys are *this* cheap!

Monique shared, "She wanted a cheeseburger. He ordered her a hamburger and they took it to his parents house to get a slice of cheese for it so he wouldn't have to pay the extra 30 cents. She called it quits. #truestory #notmystory."

4. "I like you too much to risk loving you . . . you know, because that makes sense."

Junior said, "If we keep dating we're going to end up getting married."

3. "You aren't quite my muse."

Sarah-lucy said, "When I'm with you, it makes my singing off-pitch, and singing is my job so . . . #sorry."

2. "Something just smells fishy about this . . ."

Holly shared, "In college I broke up with a guy because he smelled weird. He really did."

1. "Oh . . . yeah, I forgot about that one little detail."

Daniel tops it all off with, "'I have a fiancé I didn't tell you about . . .'"

THE MOST SELFISH REASON TO DUMP SOMEONE: THEIR RISK

"Zack," it read, "do you have a few min to chat tonight?"

The text seemed to open a trap door of marbles into my stomach.

It was from the girl I was dating at the time.

She had been waffling over some doubts about her feelings for me, and while it had been frustrating, I really liked her, so I was willing to see where things would go.

I tried to keep it casual.

"For you? How could I not???"

(I obviously tried too hard. One question mark would have sufficed.)

My mind raced with all the things I'd *rather* be doing than getting dumped (eating bees, pouring salt in my eye, rolling down a hill of porcupines . . .); but sadly, life isn't always either/or.

When we met up that night she dropped this confusing line on me:

"I don't think this is going to work out because I'm still unsure if I love you and I don't want you to wait for me to decide. I don't like that you are hurting."

"Whoah, whoah, whoah . . . you are dumping me because you *don't* love me or because you aren't sure *if* you love me?"

She thought for a second. "Well . . . what do you mean?"

"Look, if you are dumping me because you know that you don't love me or are tired of trying to figure it out, that is fine— but if you are dumping me because you don't want to hurt my feelings *if* you decide that you don't love me, well, I'm sorry, but that just doesn't work. I'm a big boy and can make my own decisions. You are worth the risk to me."

And so it is!

Discovering love is a risk—on both ends.

One must take the risk *and* be the risk. We all risk getting burned for the chance to have that fire of love ignite.

The dumbest reason to dump someone (aside from the previous ten), is because you are afraid of hurting their feelings.

Dump them because you don't love/like them, not because you *might* not in the future.

See, the other person has complete agency and can make the decision of you being a worthwhile risk or not.

But be honest with them, of course.

Give them the data they need (your feelings) to calculate their risk tolerance for you based on how they feel, but never ever ever ever run away just because you don't want to be the "bad guy" and hurt the other person *if* there is a chance that you won't love them.

That is cowardly.

That is foolish.

That is a great way to stay single. (Trust me . . . I've been on both ends of this advice.)

Because guess what?

There is a core theme in this book: dating never works . . . until it does.

And by then, there will be a battlefield of hearts, a litany of scars . . . and that is okay. That is what we signed up for to avoid living out a life of feline-filled solitude.

So don't take away the agency of another person because of your fears.

Oh, and as for that girl and me?

Well . . . she saw my point . . . *and then went on a church mission to Brazil.*

But if I am going to be dumped for another man, I'm okay if that man is God.

DON'T DUMP BECAUSE YOU'RE SCARED

You've been dating them for a few weeks. Things are going well.

You have made your list, opened up to love, met someone, planned activities around the buckets of attraction that seemed a bit shallow, and now, right when you are supposed to be feeling great—you feel sick. Not the flutters of butterflies, but the fight or flight type of feeling. Questions of doubt ground your heart.

What if I make a terrible mistake?

What if my parents hate them?

What if I hate their parents?

Basically . . . *What if I'm scared and feel I should dump them?*

Well the best thing that you should do is calm down.

It is okay to get nervous that something might work. The more it works, the more work it becomes. There will be more emotions, deeper vulnerability, and inevitably some heartbreak along the way. Relationships are scary.

When just getting into a relationship, men will typically be scared because it logically means an end of freedom while women want to progress things to the next level in an emotional way.

When getting serious about a relationship, women will typically be scared because it means so much more added pressure, while men just feel it is the next step.

Regardless of how well that describes you or not, there is one thing for sure: just because you have cold feet doesn't mean you need to amputate them or use them to run away.

There are so many reasons that things won't work out, but just as many reasons that they will.

What if you are making the best decision of your life?

What if your parents love them?

What if you love their parents?

Basically . . . *What if you're scared but work through that to find true love?*

Because yeah, relationships are scary, but so is flying. And if no one ever tried to fly, we'd still be grounded. So take heart, take wings, and have an honest chat about your fears with the person you're dating. You've got nothing to lose . . . except doubt.

MONKEY VINE SYNDROME— YOUR FEAR OF BEING SINGLE AGAIN

So I had this friend . . . you might be her.

She was kind, beautiful, and, until I met the guy she was dating, I thought she was pretty smart.

She was dating this complete dud. (No desire for school, no job, no motivation, no direction, not kind, and immature. Granted, he did have big muscles, but still).

I just couldn't help but feel that she could do so so so so so so (and one more "so") much better!

Because I loved her, I pulled her aside one day and told her that I would support her in anything she did, but that I was going to shoot her straight about her bae one time and one time only.

Her: "Go ahead."

Me: "No really . . . I'm going to tell you exactly how I feel."
Her: "I'd like that."
Me: "No you won't."
Her: "It's okay, I trust your opinion."
Me: "It isn't a good one."
Her: "I would assume not."
Me: ". . ."
Her: "Well?"
Me: "Wait . . . why would you 'assume' my opinion about him won't be good?"
Her: "Because, I mean, he's not really that good of a guy."
[Pregnant pause]
[Confused stare]
Me: "THEN WHY ARE YOU DATING HIM?!"
Her: "Because I don't have anyone else to date yet."
BWAAAAAH?!?!! My jaw dropped like the climax of a German techno song.

This phenomenon is unfortunately not unique to my friend, and if the symptom of not wanting to break up solely because you haven't found someone better describes you, then you, my friend, have "Monkey Vine Syndrome."

Monkey Vine Syndrome derives its scientific name from a monkey not wanting to let go of one vine until they are sure there is another one to grab onto. Practically, it works well for primates to survive; metaphorically, it works terribly for a more evolved species to propagate life.

Fearful of falling from the lofty platitudes of a secure relationship, these skittish souls will only vacate their vine if there is no chance of a commitment-less conclusion on the jungle floor where the pernicious predators of [dun dun DUN] singleness prey on the innocent.

In the words of the king from *The Jungle Book*, "I'm tired of monkey-ing around!"

Don't be afraid to drop dead weight and take the leap. You'll be surprised how much higher you can go.

It is okay to be single.

It is okay to be by yourself.

It is okay to not have someone be interested in you.

At times, while we are single is when we become grounded in who we are so we can get a clearer perspective to see the tree from the forest, or, in the case of my friend, an idiot from a great guy.

Remember, just because you don't have a "someone" and you aren't someone's "someone" doesn't make you a "no one."

BREAKING DOWN WHEN TO BREAK UP

You come home after a date and plop on the couch next to your roommate.

"How as the date?"

"It was my last with him."

"Wait," your roommate shouts, "You're *not* going to keep going out with him?! He's tall, good looking, super cool, solid, smart, great family, and you know he's going to be rich—what more could you possibly want?"

The condescending tone in your roommate's voice is familiar.

You mumble a response filled with certain confusion, "I mean, he's awesome, but I'm just not excited about it."

"You're getting too old to be this picky, you know."

A flush of frustration begins to bubble up, but you realize that it's true. Still, you know what you feel, even if you can't quite explain it. "I thought you told me last week that I shouldn't settle."

"Ugh. You're just broken."

We've all been there. We've been the one confused at the uncertainty, when all logic points to certainty.

We've been the roommate, exasperated at the friend dropping the person they secretly wish they could have dated.

We've even been the poor sap left in the middle of the road for no seemingly good reason wondering, "Is something wrong with me?'

This situation boils down to one question: Should I keep dating someone even if I'm not excited about them? Or in other words, **how do I settle *without* settling?**

At times, we find ourselves with those who are perfect on paper but in person something just doesn't propel you to pursue the possibility of considering them to be a potential prospect. Do you have to make the choice between finding someone that you are super excited about, but you know they might not be a good fit for you and someone who is perfect for you, but you just aren't excited about?

The answer is NO!

Imagine with me, if you will, driving down the highway of love in your relationship car. (I wonder what your scenery looks like . . . mine mostly looked like a desert.)

Like others journeying down the same highway, there are road bumps, pit stops, and even abandoned cars strewn on the side of the road.

Things are going smoothly . . . until you start to notice some issues. It starts off as a sputter, then a short power failure, then an all-out stall. You see there is a service station a few miles down and you think you might need gas (still extended metaphor here—don't get third grade on me). So you make the long hot walk there, get a can of gas, and walk back. Still not starting. *Maybe it's the battery!* You try assure yourself. So you again walk to the station, get a battery, and walk back . . . but still nothing. You try a new starter engine. Then a new alternator. And even a new . . . (hmm . . . I've run out of car parts I know. But you get the point).

On one of your trips back to the car, you see a sign that wasn't there before: "Welcome to 'The End of Your Dignity' Pop: 1."

It is there, with the car barely visible through the heat waves of your romanticization, that you realize (although it is a tough decision because you put so much time and energy into the car and tried so hard to fix it) there is a car that will take you where you need to go—and it isn't that one.

So when do you give up on a relationship?

There is a clear line when love meets self-dignity and when your desires for something better falls short of a final destination;

and it is there, my friends, you must make your stand. For at that point, it isn't true love.

Love is inspiring, uplifting, encouraging, and enlightening. Food tastes better, ambitions race higher, and reality is enlarged. And while there will be road bumps and pit stops at times, you need to fight for what you have left . . . but realize when nothing is there.

And since it is the car that is broken and not you, there is no shame in walking when the "alternator"tive is not working.

WHEN YOU DUMP

THREE REASONS THINGS FIZZLED

Wow.

They were amazing. You met at the bonfire and could hardly sleep that night thinking about them.

The next day you found them on Facebook, messaged them, and exchanged numbers. You went out on a few dates and there were just sparks like crazy. After a few dates, you even kiss!

Things are going so well . . . until one day about two weeks into this, you go to another bonfire and meet someone else. You ignore the text of the first person and slowly stop calling back as this new interest starts to envelop your thoughts.

And by the beginning of week three, the first bonfire flame is a burnt out memory, a story, and another tally when you are asked how many people you've kissed [sigh].

On the subject of falling out of love, I can't comment. I've been in love a few times and each time, the conclusion has been getting dumped or getting married. But on getting over liking someone, ah, we have volumes on that.

I've found there are typically three reasons why we fall out of like:

One: Something is off with *them*. Before you go off about this, it is important that you do this one task: write down specifically *why* you don't want to date them anymore. Share it with a couple of people and see if you really are incompatible with them or if you are victim of the second reason.

Two: Something is off with *you*. Yes, you have issues, my friend. You aren't broken and don't need fixing, but you can improve. You fake date. You look for crushes instead of foundations. You are not over that ex. You have daddy problems. Or . . . you don't think you have issues, in which case, you are in denial about your issues. (Look, we have all traveled around our own world collecting souvenirs and rocks that we carry with us—the thing is, this ain't no Southwest Airlines—baggage does not fly free. The key is to keep it under 50 lb.)

Whatever the case may be, make sure you get yourself to a point that you can let someone into your heart and life. You don't have to be perfect, but workable. I told my wife when we first met that I'm an Ikea guy—everything is more or less there, but quite a bit of assembly required. I promise it isn't as scary as people think it is . . . or so my therapist tells me.

Three: Something is off with the *relationship*. Ah, the indescribable, irrational, and irritatingly honest, "not sure why, but just don't feel right about it" thing. It really is a real thing (sometimes). And as long as you are being honest with number one and two, I would take this for a decent answer. *But beware*: if you abuse this, you will be held accountable at the last day (aka when you turn 40, are still single, and are hanging out with your weird aunt at family holiday parties).

So remember to use caution when throwing a crush into the wind. They might be your ticket to s'more than a spark.

HOW TO TAKE A BREAK WITHOUT BREAKING UP

I had a friend who was dating a super nice girl; but things weren't clicking for some reason. She was all in, but he was on the fence.

He decided that they should take a "break" instead of breaking up. I asked him the difference: "It's like when you don't talk to each other. Unless you want to . . . unless they don't, of course . . . I guess?"

People, people, people—what is this "break" mess all about? It is the worst state you can be in. You might break down when you break up . . . but to just take a "break"? *Terrible* idea. One heart is aching while the other is stringing it along. It seems odd to even call it a "break." Maybe it's actually spelled "brake"? (Ya know what, for the purposes of this section, I'll try a few different spellings and see what fits best.)

It's not progression or regression . . . it just is -gression.

I say if you are taking a brayk, give the person you are on a braik with more credit than just to tell them you need a brajck. Tell them why.

And not this, "I'm not sure" or "I prayed and don't feel right about it"—but real reasons.

So in the end, take a breijk when you are ready to end it for good and don't just lead them on—just break up.

(And after reading this over . . . none of the spellings seem to fit. They all just seem so wrong.)

WHEN TO CHAT AND WHEN TO PULL THE "FADE"

So you're done.

The relationship just is kinda . . . blah.

So do you need to have a serious sit down chat, or can you just stop calling them back?

That all depends on how serious it is.

Here is a general rule of thumb. We'll keep it simple and short.

If you have not kissed them or if you have gone on fewer than five dates, then you can pull the fade.

If you are a classy upstanding person with a good sense of self-respect and decency, then just follow what is common sense and don't run away from something you know you should do. You won't find any "make me feel better about being a jerk" sentiment in this book, my friend.

DON'T BLAME BREAKING UP ON GOD

You take your significant other on a journey to visit a very wise old man—the wisest man in the world. Not only is he wise, but he happens to know both you and your love interest.

You traverse the mountain until you arrive at his door and tell your boy/girlfriend to wait outside. They sit down and begin to anxiously bite their nails.

You go in to the wise man, "I have come to ask a question."

"Proceed," comes his response.

"Well, I was wondering if this person and I should get married. I'll do whatever you say."

Now stop . . . and think.

What do you think this wise man would tell you? If he tells you yes or no, then you can blame him for the answer and everything that is a result of that would be his fault. You are off scot-free. Wouldn't that be nice? But see, he is a wise man.

So instead he responds, "What do you think?"

"Well . . . ," you stammer, "they are nice and kind and super awesome, but I just don't really want to marry them."

"Hmm. Interesting." The wise man rubs his long beard. "That sounds about right."

"Oh thank you so so so much!" You run out with a burst of relief.

Your boo is waiting with bated breath. "And . . . ?!"

"I'm sorry, the wise man said that we can't get married."

* * *

I polled 230 people about their feelings of God directing us to break up with people.

91 percent felt that God does not meddle in breakups.

211 open-ended responses made mention that blaming God for a breakup is "bogus," a "cop out," "a crock of crazy horse [and so on]," or "letting God do your dirty work."

As for the other 19 answers? They said "In rare cases, it can happen."

Whatever you feel, I can say that this is a personal topic.
. . . especially for me.

"God" has dumped me three times.

Three.

And frankly, I'm a little tired of people hiding their fears behind prayer.

Also, I have to say, I can't believe God was so interested in making my dating life miserable that He was campaigning against me in the non-prayer hours.

I have heard many times, "It is a big decision, so *of course* God will give direction."

But there is a huge flaw in that thought because that is assuming God will give direct answers every time there is a big decision.

When I prayed where I should go to college, I got nothing.

When I prayed about starting a company, I got nothing.

When I prayed about going to get my MBA or PhD, I got nothing.

When I prayed for an answer about taking one job or another, I got nothing.

I got nothing because God was trying to give me something more important than an answer—an opportunity to choose.

I thought it out, made a decision, prayed, and then just went forward. And I made the right decision because I *made* a decision. Doesn't God care about the righteous desires of our heart?

So why do so many people blame God for breakups? Because revelation and obedience is ingrained in us. And that is wonderful! But, when we focus so much on revelation that we forget about agency, our personal freedom to choose, then we are following someone else's plan entirely.

Now, I do believe that God will intervene in some rare circumstances, but even in those cases, it is cowardly and cheap to blame it on Him. Take responsibility. It is not "God made me do this," but rather, "I don't feel good about this."

I believe that God respects our freedom to choose and so should we.

What good does it do to tell someone that God broke up with them?

Nothing.

So yes, date, pray, decide, and get an answer, but then, if the Lord has a contrary opinion, don't make yourself a martyr. For in the end, aren't we all commanded to "be wise" (Matthew 10:16) ourselves?

Now . . . a message to all those whom God "dumped:"

Don't worry.

God is not talking bad about you behind your back.

If you and He are in good standing, then don't let another's "revelation" dictate your relationship with Him.

No matter the excuse, if they don't want to be with you, they don't want to be with you and hence, you can do better. Be grateful they made the choice before you eventually had to.

YOU *BOTH* CAN DO BETTER

I have a dear friend, a best friend even, whom I love sincerely and I know she loves me as well. We have the same values, beliefs, and life goals. We work really well with each other.

We are both happily married now, but when we were single we would hang out all the time. People would always ask us why we didn't get married. We always said with a smile and a wink, "We *both* can do better."

It got a laugh about half the time and a confused "should I be offended for one of you or both of you right now" face the other half.

And while we were each other's back-up-back-up-back-up-back-up plan, I want to talk about the subtle truth of our semi-joking response.

She is an amazing woman; but my love for her remained at a gentle bubble above platonic while her love for me simmered at around the same. She deserves better because she deserves someone who will be absolutely crazy about her from the sun up to the sun down and dream of her in between. The fairy tale Disney's *UP* kind of love that everyone who hasn't found it calls nonsense and those who have found it beg for those with any sense to wait for it and work for it. And not only that, but she deserves to feel that same way about someone. The same can be said for me.

Yes indeed, **we *both* deserve better, for we deserve to love completely and be completely loved**. And we just never had that to offer to each other.

So If you are dating someone and aren't feeling it and don't want to go on . . . you deserve better. And quite frankly, so do they.

THE MEANEST THING YOU CAN BE AFTER A BREAK UP: NICE

Sometimes, the meanest thing you can be is nice.

Before I get into this I just need to say something: this section is going to be a little harsh, but I am speaking on behalf of men and not angrily to one girl. (I've already forgiven you . . . if you're even reading this . . . and based on how often you like my Facebook pics . . . you probably are.)

Girls:

You met a guy. He is super nice and you rated him a seven at first, but after a few dates found out that you actually kind of like him. You are worried that maybe he isn't the most attractive and isn't terribly social and doesn't have a solid career path, but you know that he deserves a chance and while you aren't quite over your ex, you realize that you need to move on and he is the guy that has been pursuing you. Not to mention that you just kissed and so think that you are ready to DTR into a positive place.

Guys:

The girl actually likes you. She is kind of out of your league, but she laughs at your jokes. If you can get her to like you enough before she realizes that you are a closet-gamer, then you could really make this into something special.

And time goes on . . . dating starts and maybe even a little kissing, who knows?

But there is only so long before the girl eventually feels like she is being held back and the breakup ensues.

Now is where things get awful.

The girl says that things aren't working and still wants to be friends. The guy blubbingly agrees because . . . well, what else is he supposed to say?

Then the girl takes the whole "friends" thing literally, something the guy had *no* intention of doing. She is lonely, so she calls him to talk, text, and occasionally lunch. Just to be nice.

Nice?! Seriously?

You think staying a part of his life and reminding him that he wasn't good enough for you to help you not feel lonely is "nice"?

Just leave the poor guy alone. As I've said, in three years you will be married or not talking. Stop pretending you can keep your "buddy" who really likes you when you have a husband. You are doing nothing but selfishly parading around your broken heart—which you, all by yourself, took a hammer to. You martyr yourself and make him bear the cross. You are l-i-t-e-r-a-l-l-y (not *actually* literally) killing them with kindness.

The game is a catch and release. Not catch and drag him, hook in mouth, all the way back to shore.

The only difference between your loneliness and his is that you know there isn't a chance for the future—he doesn't. **Empty hope has tried and dried more hearts a thousand times over than breakups ever have.**

So, here are Five Rules of Post-Dumping Etiquette:

1.   Do not confuse the loneliness of love's loss with the fantasies of fiction's feelings.
2.   Do not text emotional pleas.
3.   Do not call "just to check up" out of pity or even genuine interest.
4.   Do not ask out a roommate to lunch to maintain contact. If they weren't your friends before, they aren't your friends after. It is a package deal.
5.   If you do want to get back together, it will take a little more than a whiney phone call to win them over.

Non-sexist Note: The same goes for guys towards girls . . . it is just a lot more rare because the guy, well, quite frankly, the guy just forgets about the girl and finds someone else. #sorrywedontcaremore

Grammar Note: Yeah, I know that blubbingly isn't a word, you gallyfrudge.

WHAT DAY TO DUMP SOMEONE

What is a good day to dump someone?

Let me just start by saying this: *Always always* (usually) dump someone in the evening after five p.m. but before ten p.m., unless it is a Saturday. That way their day is over and then they can still come home to roommates or parents who are awake to talk about how terrible you are. Now, if you can hold out, here are the days that you should and should *not* dump someone.

Monday: *No.* Start of a week and it is tough to go through the rest of the day.

Tuesday: No. They just survived a Monday. Give them a moment to celebrate.

Wednesday: No. That is hot-tubbing time and mid-week movie night. Let them enjoy their night.

Thursday: No. There is not enough time to set up a good weekend.

Friday: *No!* Unless you are Satan, don't do it on a Friday. Completely ruins their weekend leading to a terrible week starting on Monday.

Saturday: *Only* if it is for lunch. This allows them to scramble to find people of their own gender to hang out with and go to a party to find some trick to get over you.

Sunday: *Yes!* This is such a great day to dump someone! They just had a great day of rest and can have a full four days to set up dates that next weekend.

Now . . . if you are dating an idiot, dump them Tuesday at one a.m. for all I care.

GETTING DUMPED

THREE STEPS TO GO THROUGH AFTER GETTING DUMPED

So you got dumped. Don't worry, you can do better, they didn't deserve you, yadayadayada (not as in the *Seinfeld* "yadayadayada").

But now what? What do you do *today*? *Right now*?

Can you move on? Will you ever find someone as amazing? Will you ever be able to open up again? Should you send the other person a nasty text from a different number?

There are a few definitely's in there and maybe one or two maybes; but that's not the point. The point is that now, before you decide to egg his car or ask out her roommate, you should make certain to go through the three phases of a breakup.

PHASE ONE: MEDICATE

Right after the breakup, you will need to just treat yourself.

I remember when I was introduced to Denali Extreme Fudge Chocolate Moose Tracks . . . it only comes in breakup sizes. Get some.

Also, for the first few nights, grab a few Melatonin pills and a bottle of lavender oil. Oh, and breakups are the exact reason you can get a free month of Hulu Plus.

There are always massage Groupons as well. Splurge. Find the cheapest one and then go to that spa and pay full price . . . just because you deserve it.

With social media and breakups, it might not be a bad idea to change settings in Facebook so that person doesn't show up in your newsfeed. Don't give them the satisfaction of un-friending them. WAaaaaaAAAAaY too dramatic. And don't be so quick to untag your photos. In due time.

And most importantly, don't feel bad about feeling bad. Remember, treat yourself; don't beat yourself up. Just give yourself some time.

How much time?

Well, when things weren't very serious, it once took me ten minutes (wasted three-fourths of a tub of ice cream to freezer burn). Another time it took me about three years (single handedly putting Ben and Jerry's Frozen Greek Yogurt Strawberry Shortcake back on the map).

But those are both my "too short" and "too long."

So Goldilocks, as for the "just right," simply make sure that every day, you are closer to getting over it than the day before . . . or until your subscription to Hulu Plus for free runs out. (Tip: avoid going into the Netflix free trial on the same round. Save that for the next breakup.)

PHASE TWO: MEDITATE

Once you have treated yourself . . . recalibrate. Get to know yourself again, by yourself, and take some time with just you. Once, I got all Walden and went to the woods for an entire day without speaking a single word. I even spent over an hour just following an ant. (Not a recommended method of meditation.)

Whatever your method, just take some time to relax . . .

If you can't find anything to think about, ask yourself a few simple helpful questions . . . Where are you in life? Where do you want to be? What is preventing you from being there? What do you need to get there? How can you burn off those ice cream calories?

Unhelpful questions are pretty much anything you think of during the first phase.

PHASE THREE: MEGA-DATE

Now, once you have sufficiently treated yourself with relaxation and greeted yourself into contemplation, it is time to move on. Girls, make yourself available by going to parties and telling hot guys, "We should do something together." Guys, go through your phone and find the girl that you always wanted to ask out and take her on the date of her life. Or just go out and meet people.

But beware, if you skip phase one and two and jump right to this, you will NCMO (non-committal make out). If you are wondering what that is, ask your sorry roommate where (s)he was until three a.m. the day *after* they got dumped.

Remember that these aren't stringent steps, but guidelines that have helped me and my friends through the majority of our dating lives.

FIVE REASONS THEY PULLED THE "FADE" ON YOU

Things are going great with that special someone.

The first few dates have been fun, texting has been regular, and during your last get together—I mean shoot, you even planned your next date.

Who knows, maybe you've even kissed.

Then . . . it happens.

Like a dandelion slowly floating away piece by piece . . . the inevitable demise becomes clear.

They start to become busier.

Texting back becomes rarer.

Voice message returns are nonexistent.

(Plus, who leaves voice mails . . . honestly! What is this, like, the 1700s?)

The next date is canceled the day before.

Then . . . silence.

No breakup.

No talk.

No explanation.

Yes, my friend, you've just been faded.

You have nothing left but a seedless weed of a relationship. But hey . . . it could be worse. I mean, it could have worked out.

And while you might think you are overanalyzing . . .

They might have their reasons.

You might be a bad kisser.

They might have found out about your dating blog.

You might be roommates with their ex.

They might have found someone else.

And while you might be heartbroken . . .

They might be over it.

But why do people pull the fade? Here are a few reasons:

1. They don't want to blow it out of proportion. It wasn't a big deal. You weren't official. Why make it something it never was?

2. It is too late. By the time they realized they weren't interested, it had been too long and it would have been awkward to go back and have a conversation about something that is already assumed over.

3. They are scared. They don't want to face the potential frustration.

4. You are scary. Yeah. You just may be.

5. You are imagining it. They really are just super busy right now or maybe they are in the hospital in a four-week coma and you just haven't found out so you might as well hold onto hope and keep calling and texting them because then they will finally realize that you are amazing and fall in love with you and you should definitely overanalyze it and talk about it with everyone that doesn't ask but you imagine that they do because the more you talk about it the better the situation gets. Yeah. That's probably it. Let me know how that works out for you. #harshsarcasticreality

But reasons aside, what do you do it if you are getting the fade?

Let the Three-Point Rule be your guide and move on. After all, if things are going to work out, it will be because *they* realize how much they miss you and not because you are grasping at the straws of what once could have been. That is like running around trying to catch the seeds of a dandelion flower that have been blown in a field. Great for occupying kids while babysitting, great for exercise if you don't mind looking like a moron, but alas, terrible for a metaphorical meaning of something that yields great results.

Plus, you deserve more than a weed.

CAN YOU BE FRIENDS WITH YOUR EX?

One day I was on the Internet when I came across one of the best sources of life wisdom: a meme. It showed a picture of a pretty girl and a dead dog and read, " 'I'm breaking up with you, but we can still be friends' is like saying, 'your dog died, but you can still keep it.' "

It had been a week since we broke up. While I had initiated *the* convo, it really was a pretty mutual event. But, ya know how it is . . . the feelings were pretty raw. I missed her and she, unbeknownst to me, was pretty hurt.

Since I hadn't written the section yet on being "nice" after a breakup, I called her.

[Ring, ring]

"Hello??" She sounded very irked.

"Hey you!" I cheerfully responded.

"What?"

The pointed question was dripping with irritation.

I paused, thinking she was talking to someone else, then I realized that the one-worded spear-tipped interrogation was laced with poison . . . intended for me.

". . . Oh . . . I, um, well, I just wanted to call and see how things are going and what you're up to."

"Okay. Well are you calling about my car?"

"Um, no? What do you mean?"

"Okay, well my car just broke down and my friend is coming to help out."

"Can I help?"

"Are we trying to date again?"

"Well . . . um, I just was calling to say hi and now I want to know if I can help out with your car."

[*Huge* frustrated sigh] "Zack, if you are trying to date me, fine. If you want to be my friend, I'm not interested. I have enough . . . and actually one is calling right now. Bye."

[Click]

We never spoke again.

Now, while that seemed a bit abrupt at the time, I have since realized the selfishness of my ways and been grateful for her honesty. Facebook's feature of "People You May Know" seemed to be more and more "Exes You Didn't Know Unfriended You." I was being the nice jerk after breaking up with her.

I always prided myself on being friends with exes, until I did an honest inventory. My conclusion: When the relationship has been real and sincere, friendship just is even more impossible than a regular friendship of opposite genders.

A pleasant politeness.

An appropriate appreciation.

Even a cordial Christianity.

But *not* a real relationship.

If it was a blithe bond, then don't burn a barely belabored bridge because of a breakup; but if it was something sincerely substantial, then simple social sentiments will suffice. And **while the heart misses what once was lost, the mind will be grateful to open up to new possibilities.**

So remember: If you broke up, don't selfishly sting with Cupid's broken arrows of yester-try. If you got dumped, point your attention to another target.

GET FEEDBACK AFTER A BREAKUP—BUT BE JUDICIOUS

It was the third and final time I had tried to date her over the course of ten years. We had been fantastic friends along the way because nothing ever got too serious, but she just never quite could bring herself to like me enough.

She sat me down at the end of what turned out to be our very last date. After three failed starts, she finally was ready to shoot me straight.

It was a clear target.

Ready.

"Zack, I need to just say this and make it clear . . ."

Aim.

". . . we will never work out. Does that make sense?"

Fire.

She might as well have asked for my final words after being shot.

I was a dead man talking.

And while the point hits me right in the heart, I couldn't let ten years slip away without one more thing from her.

"Can I ask you a question?"

"Zack, look, you're a great guy but really . . ." She knew I was persistent.

"Oh no. I got the picture loud and clear. You're not interested. But can I ask why you don't think it worked?"

She listed two things: I was too loud and I was too interested in entertaining her on dates instead of getting to know her.

I felt like the first was a part of me and while I could be more conscientious of my volume, I wasn't concerned with that as a character issue.

The second was absolutely spot on. I had spent my entire dates trying to put on a show when I should have been learning about her. I whole-heartedly implemented her advice and it changed the way I date for the better.

So here are the tips to getting feedback from an ex:

1. Make sure that you are close. Not some fling, but someone who really knows you and wants you to truly do better.
2. Make it timely. Don't call up weeks after a breakup, do it right after or very soon. Don't drag it out.
3. Make it about you. Don't use this time as ways to stab them. If they ask what they could do better, be gentle.

4.   Make judgments. Don't take everything they say because you aren't trying to change who you are, rather you are trying to become the best version of yourself.
5.   Get out before you make out. Few hearts have lingered without regret.

When dates don't work out, we are supposed to learn from it, right? Well, as long as you stay within these guidelines, this is a great way to expedite that process. Because we both know that there is no reason to draw this dating thing on longer than is needful. Push that flying fairy Cupid to the side and put yourself in front of the firing squad of love.

OVERCOMING DATING DISCOURAGEMENT

IT IS OKAY TO BE SAD SOMETIMES

I want to talk to the rocks. To the pillars. To the ones who are always leaned on.

Let me just say, thank you.

Thanks for being there and for being a true friend. People really do need you. Friends, family, and even strangers feel your strength and need your support to stand tall. I need you and I am so grateful for you.

With that being said, let me also say something else to you: it is okay to feel discouraged about dating.

Things don't always work out in dating . . . in fact, as you can tell from an innumerable number of failed dating stories, most of the time they don't. That can be a real thorn in your side.

I know it seems like a silly thing to say, but let me say it again, it is okay to feel discouraged. It is okay to need someone to lean on. It is okay to not be able to be strong every second of every day. You can use this as your permission slip to take a day for you. To cry. To watch a movie by yourself at home for a night. To have someone else bind up a wounded heart or lift a heavy load. You, the listener to many, may feel like there are no ears upon which your weary heart may lay its words to rest—but know that there are.

If you disagree, go under the stars for ten minutes with an open heart and tell me if you feel alone. Think of the feelings your parents had when they first held you and tell me that you are not loved. And while that may provide some comfort, it is the lifting that gets tiring.

At times the weight seems like it is too much.

At those moments, remember: it is okay to be sad. Your problems are worth being spoken. They are worth being listened to.

You can feel lonely, rejected, betrayed, and yes . . . even weak. For in those moments when you want to push away everything that makes you feel vulnerable and sad, think of what is says in the Good Book, "By the sadness of the countenance the heart is made better" (Ecclesiastes 7:3).

Yes, it will be hard at times, but you have been through hard things and guess what . . . you're still alive.

When needed, give your heart to sorrow, the forger of better men, and while you may feel a*lone*, know that you are never abandoned.

In those moments of deepest despair, there is someone who wants to hug you and say, "I'm here . . . just for you."

So never fear falling or failing—you are not forsaken or forgotten. When you fall with meekness and patience, and "wait upon the Lord," then shall you "renew [your] strength . . . [and] mount up with wings as eagles" (Isaiah 40:31) to a clearer perspective of your role, your example, and your service in the world.

And during the nights when you feel that you don't want people to thank you for your strength, but rather you just want someone to hold you in your sorrow—on those long nights, know that you have been held since the beginning (see Isaiah 46:4) and although "weeping may endure for a night . . . joy [ah, that sweet light of joy] cometh in the morning" (Psalm 30:5).

THE FIVE-STEP CURE FOR DISAPPOINTMENT

Did he never call you after that great first date? Did she never return your text? Did you lose that game? Did someone not show up to support you? Did you look into the mirror after quitting another diet? Did the business fail? Did that perfect relationship end? Did someone you care about pass away? Did a little one you were hoping to care about never make it?

Did tears make their way to your pillow at night and morning seemed forNever away? It is during those nights that it seems like the sun will never rise again.

When disappointment creeps into my heart, I try to stay positive and not unload my problems on others. But sometimes, I just need more than frozen yogurt and a hot tub. (Remember, just because others have it harder doesn't marginalize your pain.)

In thinking about disappointment, I started to analyze the etymology of the word itself:

"*dis-*" the prefix for reversal, negation, or removal.

"*-appoint-*" to assign to a position or set a time—things that have not yet occurred but are perceived future inevitabilities.

"*-ment*" the suffix for state of being.

"Disappointment," then, is the state of being the opposite of something expected.

So it would seem that the cure for disappointment is to not have any expectations so that they can never be unmet.

Ah, but no; this cannot be. We must make goals and go after them and fight with faith for that which we believe! It isn't about giving up on dreams—no, that will never be the cure. That is simply succumbing to the sickness. The cure for disappointment is not found in the avoidance, but in the acceptance; we must learn to deal with the unpreventable occasions when reality falls short of our "appointed" plans.

While my acquaintance with disappointment might not be to the personal familiarity of yours, the principles are nonetheless similar. Here is the Five-G Cure for Disappointment (they get decreasingly descriptive on purpose).

1. Get hopeful. Don't succumb to dis-courage-ment (the state of being removed from courage). Discouragement is a deadly disease distilled from the dredges of disregarded disappointment. I promise there are good things to come! Allow yourself to weather

the phases: denial, anger, and sadness. But then seek for understanding and therein you will find hope. As Shakespeare penned, "The miserable have no other medicine/ But only hope" (*All's Well that Ends Well*, act II, sc.i, l. 2). The cure is not dreamlessness, but hopefulness.

2.   Gain perspective. Pray, read scriptures, and sit under the stars for ten minutes to realize that whatever your disappointment, there is more to the universe than the pain you now feel. Look to see how you can learn, change, and grow. Usually the biggest thing that comes out of this is gratitude for all that you do have.

3.   Gather yourself. Take a (small) break. It could be hot tubbing, listening to music, running, hot tubbing, talking with a loved one, or just hot tubbing. It is important simply to know it is okay to breeeeeeeeathe.

4.   Give to others. Even if you feel broken, there are hearts that only you can mend.

5.   Go forward . . .

So in a life of "just about's" and "almost's" and "kind of's" and "nearly's" and "not quite's"—basically, in a world where things are in a state opposed to your expectations, know that there is one "G" that is constantly complete: God.

Whatever you perceive "God" to be, I know that we can reach out in prayer and experience healing, peace, and love amidst the greatest disappointments of life . . . yes, even yours. Because no matter the dark clouds of disappointment, the future still shines bright.

VULNERABILITY IS LEARNING TO LEAN, NOT JUST TO OPEN UP

We live in a world with such thick facades that often vulnerability is relinquished to late night TED talk viewing of Brené Brown as opposed to a candid exploration of emotions.

When we get dumped, we post a photo of ourselves out on the town (by ourselves).

When we get fired, we tweet about not being tied down (while waiting in line at unemployment).

When we fail an exam, we pin a pic about new doors opening (while eating Rice Krispy Treats on our bathroom floor).

But when we post that we had a tough day, we get unfriended.

So today, I hope you will take a leap of vulnerability with me. After going through some particularly challenging times in my life, I learned that **the real key to vulnerability is not telling someone you fell, but allowing them to help you get up.**

Yes, vulnerability is not just opening up to someone, but leaning on them . . . not asking for an ear, but asking for support . . . not posting for likes, but pleading for love.

That is tough.

Story time:

A few years ago I was really hurt by someone. I was supposed to fly across the country to go on a date with them. We had gone out a bunch and things were going really well. She even texted me the morning I was flying out to tell me how excited she was.

Unfortunately, she stood me up to make out with an ex-boyfriend. No call, no text, and she didn't even answer the door when I went to pick her up.

I couldn't help it.

I cried.

Not like a "Susan Boyle YouTube video watch for the 50th time" type good cry . . . but like a "this is hard and I'm going to stay single forever" type cry— you know, the Adele kind.

Do you know where I went?

To my grandma.

. . . my dead one.

Yeah.

I went to my grandma's grave.

My deceased grandmother was the only one whom I trusted enough to hear me cry. (This, by the way, is not saying anything about my friends, but about myself.)

But don't we all do that?

Don't we shy away from the real emotions lest we are perceived as being a downer or an emotional leech or maybe worse . . . needy [gasp]?!

And guess what?

It is okay to admit you aren't perfect. It is okay to just be you—even if you feel you aren't quite strong enough to admit you are weak. For when you are weak, you are willing to do what you need to do improve; hence, you are making you strong.

Now for those brave almost ADD souls who are still reading this book, a message: *You are loved. You are cared about. You are known. There are those who* want *to support you—let them.*

When words are too scary to say and trust is too fragile to give and hearts are too soft to share—it is at that moment that you are understood most. And when you feel alone and don't want to lean on someone, let that become a springboard to make you better. Push on that wall of fear so hard, with the help of your friends, family, and God, that it is pushed over into a ramp to launch you up to a better version of you.

Yes, **true vulnerability turns walls into ramps.**

DATING MINDSET: REGARDLESS OF REJECTION, FORGET REGRET

From personal experience, I can say that one in three dates have not worked out.

Either the girl has turned me down, canceled last minute, or stood me up (but at least I earned SkyMiles on that last one, eh?).

I know many guys who stop asking women out and women who stop trying to get asked out. It is hard and depressing at times.

It is at those times that you must remember that it will eventually work out. As it has been said, "Everything works out in the end. If it hasn't worked out yet, then it's not the end" (Tracy McMillan, *I Love You and I'm Leaving You Anyway*, 2010)

One time I went to a seminar of the popular motivational speaker Tony Robbins, where he had us think how we were feeling at that exact moment. I thought to myself, "Fine."

He then asked us to celebrate as if our favorite sports team won the world championship. The room erupted in cheers. I noticed my mood improve to "Great!"

Then . . . the music began. An intense beat of a crazy dance song that began to get louder and louder and louder. He then said, "Now take that energy you put into celebrating and on the count of three, multiply it by ten!"

"One . . ."

The music grew louder.

"Two . . ."

The anticipation was palpable.

"THREE!!!"

It was complete pandemonium!

Chairs were getting thrown around, mosh pits began, the music was screaming, some guy next to me smashed his iPad, and I ended up on someone's shoulders running around like a mad man.

Then he yelled, "STOP!" A breathless gasp of chaos was calming as everyone took their seats. When our attention was focused on him once again, he whispered, "*Now* . . . how do you feel?"

I felt like I could fly!

And then he said something I'll never forget, "And how about that? Nothing in the world changed in the last five minutes besides your *perspective*. The positive attitude to succeed is completely up to you!"

I thought about that a lot in starting businesses and dating. When things get tough, we must look to and imagine ourselves succeeding eventually. That will help keep us positive and ready to move forward, regardless of how bad things may seem.

Don't let dating defeat you.

Dating doesn't define you.

Regardless of rejections, forget regret.

Truly, your mind-set, not your circumstances, will move you forward.

Zack Oates

DEAR GIVING OLDER SINGLES A HARD TIME

Dear Giving Older Singles a Hard Time,

Chances are, this letter is either to you or from you.

If it is to you, let me just say that I hope you don't take offense. My intention is not to be hurtful, but to explain to how your words have hurt others—and most likely with the best of intentions.

Who are "we?"

We are those that are single and above the "normal age" to marry. We aren't gay. We don't have porn problems. We aren't bitter about our divorce. We aren't obsessed with our careers. And we aren't having too much fun. We just happen to be over 21 and not married. #puttingtheSINinSINGLE

You see, so many times, you offer help, but it just doesn't come across very well. We don't need set-ups with weird friends (unless we are the weird friend, then keep it coming), overstated advice (we've heard it, know it, tried it, and are reading a book right now about it), comments about us being selfish, text messages when someone mentions the *Bachelor* or *Bachelorette*, you telling us we are "stupid" when we break up with someone, or a constant barrage of "why are you single?"

And most important (outside of a hospital), no one ever needs to be asked, "What is wrong with you?"

Ever. [Period]

Now, what we do need is your support, love, kindness, understanding, and sincere friendship.

Instead of incessantly indicating the individual intention that has been thus far elusive (a spouse), help us to see all that we have accomplished. Don't dwell on the one failure (as you see it); shed a light on the many accomplishments (as we should see it). I'm not asking you to be a patronizing cheerleader, but rather I'm reminding you of you when you were single.

When we go to sleep at night, we are woefully aware that we are single. And in those dark moments, often your question echoes in the chambers of an empty heart, "What is wrong with me?"

Well nothing is wrong with us.

We are working and we will get "there" (whatever that "there" happens to be for us), but coming down on us for being single doesn't help us get "there" any better.

Now, you may say this is unfair of us since we poke fun of ourselves. We put up our single life on the altar of easy jabs. We make the topic our target. But that target is really our shield. See, your comments pierced us a few times and we realized that there was no way to avoid it. So we put up a target as our shield—at least this way, we know it is coming. But it doesn't mean that words never get through.

Some say that we are thinking of ourselves, we are too picky and that we are having too much fun. But if you saw the million rides we give to the airport, the long nights of comfort that are given, the hours spent working on serving others; if you saw the dreadful red flags of our dating pool, the emotionless first dates, the amount of people that we like who don't like us at the same time; and oh, if you saw the aching hearts, tears, and long nights of begging for comfort—if you saw all that (or maybe remembered), we think you would have a different perspective. And if you have lived through all of this, all the more reason for kindness before critique.

Know we are trying. We are trying to learn charity, trying to be open, trying to find the right person, trying to be the best person we can, and trying to distract ourselves occasionally because no, loneliness is not fun. And maybe marriage and parenting isn't going to be this fairy-tale awesomeness, but let's all just lift each other up in whatever station we may be. We all have crosses that are barely bearable, but I feel we were put here to lighten the load, not add to it.

So before we finish, let me tell you why we're even telling you this.

We wish we could say that your words don't matter . . . but they do, because we look up to you. And even when words unintentionally cut, we know you want us to have an amazing family and want to help us get there.

Your love means so much, which is why we thought you might like to know how we feel.

Sincerely,

Honestly Trying

PS. Let's not make this awkward or dramatic. We aren't breaking up with you—just thought our relationship needed a touch of honesty.

YOU ARE WORTH BEING LOVED

All humans go through heartache. I'm not talking about the kind where a good make out and an hour of Fail videos will heal—but real hurt. The kind that makes you fear being tender. The kind that makes you put up transparent walls (looks like you're open, until someone comes close). The kind that makes you wonder if you are worth it . . .

That is the "storm after the calm" type hurt.

That is the "loneliness after love" type pain.

See, when you're in love, you feel that you are at your best. *Everything* is better. The air fresher, food more savory, and life more livable. You believe in yourself because the one person in the world who knows you best . . . well, they believe in you too. Ultimate vulnerability juxtaposed beside seemingly unstoppable strength.

Then, somehow (all of the time until the last time) . . . it ends.

And the devil inside takes the stage.

With a merciless monologue, the bitter limelight dims on him.

'You knew it would end!'

'I told you not to let that person in. Why don't you listen?'

'If you can't be loved at your best, how can you be loved at all?'

Insecurities fill sunken seams left in a torn heart. And slowly, you begin to build the base for barriers of belief. Higher and higher they climb until the shadows block a belief in yourself.

But don't worry, for on the surface, life continues. Maybe you don't even see the walls or know they are there . . . until you, brick by brick breaking down those barriers, can love again.

And so to all of you who have lost, to all of you who are afraid to lose, and to the few who don't want to find out what it is like to gain:

You are what's worth it.

Just . . . you.

As you are.

Not in a way that the shampoo commercials mean it, but really.

Not because of someone is interested in you or the business you start or the trophies you earn. Not because of the hair you have or the sales you made or the friends you have. And certainly not because of the people you know or the followers on Twitter or the position in your church or the abs you have (because you have them. Keep in mind a six pack is like the sun, it is always there, but sometimes it is just a bit cloudy) . . .

While none of those things are bad, and many are inherently good, know that they are not what comprise why you are worth it.

You are worth it because many eons ago, you were created by a Heavenly Father who thought you were worth it. A couple thousand years ago, His Son came to earth and agreed with Him. And right now you are taking a breath that should be a reminder that those two events happened, for your sake, just for you. Because *you* are what's worth it.

And while you can be better, you are enough.

Instead of worrying about your lost love, or losing love, or maybe being someone's loss—love yourself. Because you are worth loving.

So in a life filled with broken dreams, know that you, yes . . . even you—especially you—are worth it.

LOVE IS THE GOAL

GIVE UP NOW—YOU WILL *NEVER* STAY MARRIED TO THE SAME PERSON

I have a devoutly religious friend. She married her equally religious high school sweetheart after waiting for him on his two-year mission and dating him for two more years. They were married for five years . . . before he filed for divorce and became an atheist.

My parents got engaged five days after their first date in 1981. They are still married.

What . . . what?!

How does that happen? I thought it was so important to know someone before you marry them and then everything works out?

Well . . . not quite.

See, after a few basic traits of "must haves" and "can't haves" for the sake of compatibility, the person you marry is of little to no consequence.

Why?

Because they aren't the person you will stay married to.

In a study done by a Harvard psychologist Dr. Dan Gilbert ("The Psychology of Your Future Self," TED Talk posted June 2014), he interviewed thousands of individuals about personal change and concluded that "all of us are walking around with an illusion, an illusion that history, our personal history, has just come to an end, that we have just recently become the people that we were always meant to be and will be for the rest of our lives." That is because it is easier to look back and see the changes that have happened than it is to look into the future and imagine inconceivable circumstances that will surely shape us.

That "illusion" that *we* have already done most of our changing in life is as scientifically and rationally ridiculous as the "illusion" that we are marrying someone for the rest of our lives.

I, for one, have spent so much time trying to find "this specific type of girl," while completely ignoring the fact that she will be different in five years, ten years, and fifty years . . . and guess what? So will I.

And if marriage is a commitment, then, in effect, I have to choose to stay committed and married to a new person, *as a new person*, every day.

That choice is made by work.

When I was single, I was afraid of staying married to one person forever. Seemed boring. But that fear was completely unfounded based on the fact that I will never marry one person.

I'm not saying that my friend is to fault and my parents are to emulate.

Not at all. There are so many circumstances I can't even pretend to understand about why one couple is together and the other isn't.

What I *am* saying is that **we only have one choice . . . and that is to continually choose to be married to the same new person over and over.**

And that, to me, is a lot less scary than I feared. (Actually, it sounds quite nice.)

So after looking for compatibility, love and marriage is about finding someone who is committed to change *with* me as we constantly become new. For in the seas of change, commitment is the only sure foundation to which we can anchor our relationships.

COMPANY MAKES A PARTY

It is important for things to be natural, not so calculated!

It was a normal summer day. I was dating a girl.

We sent a few benign texts back and forth about a couple of funny occurrences that day and then decided to meet at a pizza shop for dinner at eight p.m.

My departure time of seven forty-five seemed to stretch on endlessly into the ticks of the library clock. Finally, our date began.

I got there early to make sure we would have a table and so that she didn't have to wait in the lobby alone.

We sat down and got a pie (pepperoni, not pumpkin . . . again, I'm from Jersey) to share with a couple of root beers. We talked, laughed, held hands over the table, played footsies under the table, learned about our waiter's new son (and yes, it did work and he got extra tip . . . exploiter) and smiled at each other in silence.

Then we went back to her apartment and I helped her with homework (or rather sat there while she did it) until about eleven thirty when she walked me to my car and was in bed by midnight.

That was it.

The best date I had ever had up until that point.

Pizza. Homework. Done.

I experience the same phenomenon with my wife now. Going to the grocery store is genuinely something I look forward to.

I've spent hundreds of dollars on a single date, an evening listening to Boyz II Men on the beaches of Italy that was planned for weeks . . . but really, in the end, it's the company that makes a party. No trying, no games, no calculation . . . just the right company.

One thing that I *do* know about love is this: no matter how terribly things are going in life, if you have someone whom you love that loves you, deep down you know that everything will be okay.

The best date ever isn't about the *date* at all, it is about *your* date.

LOVE IS ORGANIC—NOT PERFECT

One question that a lot of people have asked me is, "What qualifies you to talk about dating?"

Well, I have failed in almost every way at dating. And I wish I could say that I feel sorry for myself, but it was the path that led me to my current state and I would gladly travel those tear-soaked trails again to get where I am now.

After all the attraction-ary arithmetic, there is an unsolvable solution of love.

That is what this all boils down to.

In my quest to deduce love to a systematic procedure to guard my heart, I have realized that you will never have a perfect ten out of ten (meaning that the five buckets you each have are completely filled). There will be different levels of each type of attraction, timing may not be just on, and things may seem a bit off. We learn in the movie *Good Will Hunting*, "You're not perfect, sport, and let me save you the suspense: this girl you've met, she's not perfect either. But the question is whether or not you're perfect for each other."

An imperfect series of attractions and timing can still lead to the perfect love. For love is organic. If you want a rose, you don't plant a seed and the next day reach into the dirt and rip up a flower. You plant, water, care for and . . . eventually . . . it is a rose.

So in the final analysis, while I was looking for physical, intellectual, emotional, spiritual, and sexual attraction at the same time keeping a pulse on the timing of the situation . . . I really was looking for none of that. **I was just looking for someone that I can love who is crazy enough to love me too.** For now I really do believe that I've found someone who doesn't just love me despite my random rants and quirks . . . but because of them.

After all, don't we all deserve that?

LOVE ISN'T MAGIC, IT'S BETTER—IT'S REAL

A few years ago, I began to feel that true lasting love in marriage is like the tooth fairy.

It was like some big joke that everyone is in on . . . except me. Like you all think it's so cute when I write about believing that love is real . . . and what's more, that it will happen to me! I was feeling pretty tricked. Truman Burbank'ed, if you will (If you get that reference without Google, give yourself a point.)

But the more I thought about it, the more I realize that true lasting love really *is* like the tooth fairy.

See, when I was about seven years old, I lost one of my baby molars. I was pumped for payday and knew that the tooth fairy was coming that night.

This time, I was determined to stay awake and try to convince her to give me more money, since it was a bigger tooth, after all.

It only made cents (and dollars).

About an hour into my waiting, the door creaked open and I heard the "tooth fairy" start to creep into my room. I burst out of bed and said, "HI!"

Much to my surprise, it was . . . my dad. He jumped and dropped ten dollars in singles on the floor. Ironically the same amount he thought I might get earlier that night.

Or is it not *ironic?!* My young mind raced as my innocence hopelessly started to slowly slip between my frail fingers.

My childhood was lost. The tooth fairy wasn't a magical beautiful lady . . . it was a fat hairy offensive lineman.

Hmm. Not quite what I was expecting.

And that is how I felt about lasting love in marriage. I have always imagined it to be this magical wonderful thing that is a constant Disneyland (minus the kids) experience. But I've come to realize that it is different . . . and that is okay.

I still believe in the tooth fairy and I believe in love.

It might be different than I expected, *but the reward will be the same.*

You will find love if you haven't. You will grow love if it is fleeting. You will regain love if it is lost.

Just try it with me.

Let's have a little faith. I think we can at least try. Maybe not faith in the delivery method . . . but for sure in the reward.

Because while I was devastated the tooth fairy wasn't real, I still got my ten dollars, and that bought enough candy to make me forget all about it.

A CLASSIC TALE: TINDERELLA MEETS MR. RIGHT (SWIPE)

In 50 years from June 28, 2014, a bright-eyed ginger grandchild is going to sit at the feet of my cousin during a family gathering of her and her husband's golden anniversary and ask, "How did you and Grandpa meet?"

"Well, once upon a time . . . ," she will proceed to tell a big flaming lie. (A story of a blind date will do just fine.)

After all, how is this young child in 2064 even going to understand a smartphone, an app, and especially *Tinder*???

Yes, my cousin and her husband met on Tinder. I went to their wedding and it was a beautiful ceremony filled with family, love, and two very excited over-dated-now-former singles.

In my reflection on each of our fairy tales, I realized that our glass slipper often slips between our fingers and our knight in shining armor gallops past as we are sitting and waiting for . . . for . . . well . . . for something else.

What else, though?

Why not Tinder? Why not a blind date? Why not long distance? Why not a leap of faith?

Because it is not what we thought it would be. It isn't "Godot" enough. Well we can wake up from that dreamland right now because it hardly ever is Godot enough.

Let's think about the real people in your life that are in love. How did they meet? What was their courtship like? How did they feel about each other when they first met?

If you don't know . . . ask them!

What I think you'll find is that love happens when people aren't expecting it because when we are looking too hard, we over analyze and aren't our true selves.

And this goes far beyond just love. Look back at some of the best things that have happened to you in life and tell me, how often did those things come about exactly how you thought they would? Personally, it has been very very few. I have been so blessed by the unexpected when I have embraced and allowed some of the most amazing unplanned moments to interrupt my schedule.

I haven't found any magic beans, but the seeds of relationships grown organically have grown into something that I could have never fabricated through a calculated dating game. They happened in spite of, or despite, my efforts.

So if your heated relationships have fallen cold and now you have a burning urge to fuel the fire of love—find a potential match, strike up a conversation, and see if there are sparks to kindle a potential flame . . . even if it is on Tinder.

For in the end, waiting for what you are expecting can't hold a candle to a 50-year start on a true happily forever and ever after.

BETTING ON A LOVE MORE THAN POO

A girl came over a few years ago and we were just chatting in my kitchen.

She asks to use the restroom.

(A gamble as it is.)

She chose the loo that was separated from the kitchen by only a thin door. Needless to say she rolled the dice and lost.

Things got . . . loud.

:/

I turned on some music to give her privacy, but it wasn't enough for my skittish self. I yelled through the door that I needed to do something upstairs. A few minutes later I hear a flush . . . then another . . . then a third. Now look, I'm mature and old enough to know that girls have "that time of the month" when they poop. I get it. I do.

But three flushes . . . ?

Hmm.

So I come back down to check on everything and she is standing there looking a little shifty and says, "So . . . this is kinda awkward . . . but there is no plunger in your bathroom."

"Oh . . ." I tried to be as normal as possible.

A little jiggle of the handle and some non-romantic (but very aromatic) candles did the trick.

We fixed the problem and carried on.

Buuuuut, besides the fact that she asked me if I was going to write about that story on my blog, it brought some really interesting thoughts to my mind.

A good friend gave me some great insight on love. She said that she is not looking for a guy who wants to run a business or is a male model or a pro at a cocktail party, but rather someone where there is lasting love—not a crush or infatuation, but love. The kind of love where, when he is sick because he was up all night with a kid throwing up and she has the flu and is going out both ends and the teenage daughter has been grounded for weeks (much more painful for parents, I realize now) . . . she could leave the house and kiss him on the forehead and know that the love is real.

A real love transcends all of that because it is more than all of that.

Because I realize that sometimes life isn't all the colors of the rainbow. Sometimes it can be crappy. But when the chips are down (I don't really get that reference, but I am assuming it has to do with poker and I'm pretty sure I'm using it right), and you are starting to feel a tinge of weltschmerz, you know that they've got your back . . . sometimes literally.

One little boy said, "Love is when my daddy has to wipe my mom's butt after she goes to the bathroom because she broke both her arms."

So that is the love I think we should look for or work to cultivate. Not the crapshoot fairy tale love but a love more real.

A love more than the mundane of life.

A love more than the superficial.
Ah yes, even a love more than poo.

BE BRAVE ENOUGH TO LOVE

Are you brave enough to love?

I mean think about it . . . to love is one of the bravest decisions that a human can make in life with the biggest payoff that a human can receive. But really though, anyone can take a bullet and die for someone; but to truly love and live for someone is entirely different. To love is to give someone full permission, accessibility, and even ownership to your heart. That takes courage. You are basically giving someone else a piece of you and telling him or her, respectively, that you entirely trust them to do with it what they will. Would you give someone your left arm? Your foot? Your head? It seems ridiculous—yet, the giving of one's heart is nothing short of divinely natural.

And while there is much risk involved and fear inherent in the quest of love, in the words of George Sand, a French author, "There is only one happiness in life, to love and be loved" (Letter to Lina Calamata, 1862).

From the opening line of *Twelfth Night* comes the acclamation, "If music be the food of love, play on" (Act 1, sci. 1).

So on we play, with the hope that all will end on a good note, with the hope that the sting of love won't be too sharp and that the thrill of love won't be too flat. And while we hope to fall into love with a sure step and gentle catch, it doesn't always work out that way.

A wise religious leader said,

> One of the grand errors we tend to make when we are young is supposing that a person is a bundle of qualities, and we add up the individual's good and bad qualities, like a bookkeeper working on debits and credits.
>
> If the balance is favorable, we may decide to take the jump [into marriage]. . . . The world is full of unhappy men and women who married their mates because . . . it seemed to be a good investment.

Love, however, is not an investment; it is an adventure. And when the marriage turns out to be as dull and comfortable as a sound investment, the disgruntled party soon turns elsewhere for adventure. . . .

Entering a marriage calmly and rationally is like dancing a bacchanal calmly and rationally; it is a contradiction in terms. It takes into account everything except what is important—the spirit. (Gordon B Hinckley, "Love and Marriage," *Deseret News,* October 18, 1977)

How does you know if it is love?

In my opinion, love is serving and giving for the sake of the other's joy. Or, in the words of John Milton in *Paradise Lost,* "Freely we serve,/ Because we freely love, as in our will/ To love or not; in this we stand or fall" (Indianapolis: Hackett Publishing Company, 2005, 163 V. line 538–40).

And if you have any doubts about how brave you have to be to love, just ask Superman, Spider-Man, Batman, and most other superheroes that are single—some things just seem too dangerous.

Remember: **Love is kind, but it isn't free. Your risk is the payment. A potential of forever is the reward.**

WORK: THE WAY YOU'LL KNOW IF YOU STILL LOVE YOUR SPOUSE

A few years before I met my wife, I realized I had been lying to myself . . . I had been dating to date, dating to cure boredom, dating to spend time with fun people and, occasionally, even dating to just have a good story.

But whatever I was doing, I certainly wasn't dating to marry, as I had been professing.

An endless procession of tidy first dates would do the trick to keep the facade while hiding the fear.

When I realized this, I asked myself what my big fear was. What was keeping me from opening up?

And the answer was quite simple.

You see, I was afraid of falling *out* of love.

I was afraid of succumbing to the fate of so many around me. The rough bumps and ends to marriage inundated my social media while the low-lit bits of lasting love were locked in the layers of mild moments and simple smiles for which words seem too inadequate and public proclamations too cheap. I was barraged with the tough and blind to the tender.

So I set out to change my perspective, my heart, and my fear.

With so many of my friends that have gone through so much heartache after faltering and failed marriages, I began my quest to find the magic hidden in marriage—understanding that it is never a fairy tale. I set out to ask married people two simple questions:

1. "What is the key to a successful marriage?"
2. "How do you know you still love your spouse?"

I asked newlyweds of a week, widowers who had been married for over 60 years, taxi drivers, grandparents, my parents, friends—everyone whose ear I could borrow. All in all, I have asked over 100 people.

To the first question on a successful marriage I got the same answer over and over and over: **the key to a successful marriage is work**. Work to serve the other, work to keep things exciting, and work to show appreciation . . . wonderful work.

The answer to the second question about how they know if they still love their spouse surprised me. All of the answers boiled down to one word:

Work.

Work was the answer to both questions.

"Work . . . ?"

Work.

For after the butterflies flew away and there was nothing left but barren cocoons of a passionate memory, many people wondered where the love went. Almost every single interview mentioned this moment of feeling like they "lost" the love. Many of these people worked to find it and discovered that love hadn't flown away, but it moved. (Some who got divorced realized it wasn't what they wanted after they found it, but that is an entirely different book.)

It moved from getting love to giving love. It evolved and matured from a fleeting fluttering feeling to a candid concrete commitment. It took work to find it and it took work to keep it.

Those people who still loved their spouse said they knew it because they still worked at it, *even though, at times, they didn't want to.*

So I began to wonder, *What is work in marriage?*

It has been said, "A happy marriage is not so much a matter of romance as it is an anxious concern for the comfort and well-being of one's companion" (Gordon B. Hinckley, "What God Hath Joined Together," *Ensign*, May 1991).

One of the greatest guys I know who has one of the best marriages I've seen told me his secret: "As a married couple, we need to keep doing those little special things we did when we were dating . . . compliments, spontaneous dates, and fun make out sessions." Work requires time and energy.

Or as a famous inspirational speaker said, "marriage isn't any big thing, it's a lot of little things. Acts of kindness every day create a happy marriage" (John Bytheway, *What We Wish We'd Known When We Were Newlyweds*, Bookcraft, 2000).

Work also consists of staying true. When questions arise and fuzzy feelings of newlywed bliss are fleeing, it is then that loyalty is more important than love. **For love will get you married, but loyalty keeps you married.**

Those who know they love their spouse still work at it.

If you are searching for love, work to find it.

If you have love, work to keep it.

Do you have a dream to make a wonderful marriage your reality? I am starting to discover that it comes down to another one of Gordon B. Hinckley's beautiful thoughts, "Work is the miracle by which . . . dreams become reality" (Standing for Something [New York: Times Books, 2000], 80).

Don't worry . . . things will work—if you do.

THE GREATEST THING YOU'LL EVER LEARN

It was my grandfather's 80th birthday. He was starting to slow down, but he couldn't be kept down by any stretch.

And just to tell you a little bit about Granddad Reid: he's had three bouts of cancer, three strokes, and two heart attacks (give or take a few life-threatening challenges) and still plays tennis . . . needless to say, he's a total boss.

At his dinner party, his kids each got up to say something nice about him . . . then he stood up. When he took the microphone to give an impromptu speech of his life's advice, everyone got a little nervous. After all, there were (great) grandchildren there.

But he did something that no one expected—after a few seconds of silence . . . just standing there . . . he started to sing. Now most of you are probably too young to have grandparents who remember this song, but he started off, "There was a boy, a very strange enchanted boy . . ." It was at this point that his kids rushed up to him and told him not to sing but just to say something.

The song that he began was Nat King Cole's "Nature Boy." And I wish he would have sung the whole song, because I don't think that was Granddad being a crazy old guy, but I think he wanted to get to the end message of that song.

Because the last line is, **"the greatest thing you'll ever learn, is just to love and be loved in return."**

For a guy who was turning 80 and who had kissed death his fair share, maybe that was exactly what he was trying to say.

When you love and aren't loved it's exciting but depressing.

When you are loved and don't love it's flattering but annoying.

When you love and are loved the world turns just for you . . .

Love and be loved! Is there a greater thing you can learn through experience?

Hopefully, 60 years from now, I can look at a room of posterity—companion at my side—and say the same.

TRUE LOVE ISN'T A FAIRY TALE—IT *DOES* EXIST!

Death was slowly reaching out his shaky fingers toward my Great Uncle Paul.

This dear man, a silent example of charity, was nearing the end of his year-long, bed-ridden battle with a degenerative nerve disease in his home—a home he built with his own hands for his barely budding family ages earlier. His body was feeble, and his words were scarce. In fact, he would say maybe three or four sentences a day.

I tried to visit him and his sweet wife, Della Mae, as often as I could—always finding myself a better person when I left for just being around their fairy-tale-like love (some people just have that effect on others, I guess).

When I stopped by one day, almost a week before he passed away, I had a life-changing experience (completely unexpected, as most are).

Della Mae was busily tiding up the living room around Paul's bed. Unassumingly, quietly, and deliberately, Paul raised his gentle hand a few inches from the sheets where it lay.

"Della Mae . . ." It was too quiet; she didn't hear. He rattled out a raspy cough. "Della Mae . . ."

She turned and rushed to his side, eager to accomplish any need of her beloved spouse.

"Yes, Paul?" she cheerfully asked.

I assumed he wanted something to eat, or some medicine, or just have his pillows rearranged.

But what he said surprised me. And his words forever changed me.

"I love you, and you're beautiful." That was it. Six words.

Her cheeks turned a deep shade of rose, and a tender laugh escaped her lips. It was so effortless and genuine—the kind of chuckle where you don't even realize you laughed until you are trying to remember minutes later why you are still smiling.

"Oh Paul! I love you too, dear!" With a soft kiss on his forehead, back she went to work, this time a little more slowly.

Before I left, I asked Della Mae how often Paul would express his love like that. Her response touched me: "Every day since we've been married."

Now, before I was married, I was at times cynical about love. We all are sometimes. But underneath all of my adventure and hyped-up social media posts, there was just a kid waiting—waiting for that moment when the word "love" could freely fly off my tongue with uncalculated kindness and not be limited by this life or by the barricades of past hurt.

And now I've found it. It isn't the magical kind of love in a Nicholas Sparks book, but it is real, abiding, deep, and genuine.

So yeah, I believe in love.

I believe I can work to make that love just like Paul and Della Mae's.

A kind of love that grows stronger with every loving word that is shared between a husband and wife. A kind of love that transcends death and knows no bounds.

So today, right now—before a page turn, let's commit to the quest for the unquenchable adventure of the possibility of our "happily ever after." That is the kind of quest that takes work, daily service, and unabated affirmations of affection. That is the kind of quest worth fighting for. And that is the kind of quest that allows love to find its way into the pages of your own fairy tale.

PARTING CONCLUSION

IF YOU ONLY READ *ONE* SECTION, READ THIS LAST PIECE OF ADVICE

W e hear "don't settle for less than the best," but "don't expect perfection."

We hear "you have to give a little," but "don't change for someone."

We hear "don't play the dating game," but "go out with lots of people."

We hear "go and flirt," but "don't be too forward."

Basically, if you ask two people the same question about dating, you'll get at least three different answers.

I was challenged to bring this entire book to a single section. Here's what I would say:

1. Give yourself a chance. Be open to the possibility of love.
2. Give someone else a chance. Date someone looking for reasons that it will work out and not just why it won't. Give a relationship an honest shot by removing as many distractions as possible. Choose to love.
3. And the most important piece of advice I can give: don't take other people's advice.

That's right.

Don't take dating advice.

I've chosen to not talk about the story of my wife and me until this point for a very particular reason: I didn't follow my advice.

Yes, the only time it was right was when I did everything wrong. I don't know if it worked out despite or because of my blunders, but it worked.

Three months before I was moving out of the state, we met on a big singles camping trip to southern Utah on a hike and struck up a conversation. It turned out that we had over 100 mutual friends and had never met before. We kissed for the first time later that day and were together constantly for the remaining two days of the camping trip. We went out as soon as we got home. I canceled three dates that I had scheduled. We called and texted multiple times a day. Five days after we met, I invited her to come to a family reunion that was fourteen hours away in a car. She skipped her best friend's wedding in which she was a bridesmaid (with her best friend's approval, by the way) to come. A couple days after returning home, she left for a month on a backpacking trip through Asia. I decided to not date anyone else. The day after she returned, we became exclusive and less than two weeks later, I proposed. When I got on my knee, pulled out the ring, and asked, "Will you marry me?" it was the first time we had *ever* spoken about marriage. She said yes and the rest is history (and if we constantly work at it, the future too).

So follow your heart, but just don't leave your head behind. And keep going. Failure in dating means your one step closer to success—not just marriage, but happiness. Michael Jordan, arguably the best player in the history of the NBA said, "I've missed more than 9,000 shots in my career. I've lost almost 300 games. Twenty-six times I've been trusted to take the game winning shot and missed. I've failed over and over and over gain in my life. And that is why I succeed" ("Failure," Nike commercial). We succeed because we keep going, not because we failed along the way.

And remember that the point of a first date is not to decide if you will be happy in 50 years rocking on the porch as your grand-kids run around—no. The purpose of a first date is to figure out if you want to go on a second date. The purpose of a second date is to decide if you want a third. And, in my case, the purpose of a third date is to propose.

True love is like a snowflake—no, not because it disappears when you touch it, but because it is unique to every situation. And when you are taking someone else's advice, it is from *their* perspective and what *they* would do. But guess what, the person you are dating isn't interested in *them;* they're interested in *you.* Now before you go off demanding a refund on a book about dating advice that finishes with a bogus lesson like this, let me explain. You shouldn't follow every piece of advice in this book, but rather think about which ones feel best to you and implement those.

So don't do what your friend would do or your mother or your brother or me . . . or quite frankly even yourself as you are. **Do what the *best version* of you would do.**

For you are pretty great.
You are worth being loved.
You are worth finding love.

So don't get down that dating hasn't worked for you yet—because dating never works . . . until it does. And while it may take you a thousand dates to find your love, when you do, everything will be worth it.

> Be yourself. Especially, do not feign affection. Neither be cynical about love; for in the face of all aridity and disenchantment, it is as perennial as the grass . . . And whatever your labors and aspirations, in the noisy confusion of life, keep peace in your soul. With all its sham, drudgery and broken dreams, it is still a beautiful world. Be cheerful. Strive to be happy. (Max Ehrman, *The Desiderata of Happiness* [New York: 1995], 10).

BONUS: GREAT DATE IDEAS

While company makes a party and the person is the most important aspect of a date, here are a few go-to date ideas that I've used. Remember, while most dates include food and an activity, first dates should be less than two hours. Also, keep in mind that whether you are on a first date or married for 50 years, the purpose of a date is to get to know each other better, have fun, and create mutual memories.

So, here are some ideas that you have full permission to pawn off as your own.

1: SWEET ARCADE

Keep it simple. Keep it fun. Grab some frozen yogurt and then get in touch with your inner kid with some video games and laser tag. Try to play games where you are on the same team.

2: LAWN GAMES IN THE PARK

Go get a croquet set (or bocce ball, lawn darts, corn hole, ladder ball, or some other outdoor game) and go to the park to play. It is super fun and a simple way to start great discussions. Bring cupcakes and a blanket to really step things up.

3: LIGHTS AT NIGHT

Get glow sticks. Shake them up. Make paper airplanes. Break open the glow stick and cover the paper airplanes and have a contest from the top of a building or mountain to see who can throw their plane the farthest. (If you are playing lawn games in the park, try to break glow sticks on the balls/darts as well) Bring a lot of paper to try multiple times and be sure to clean up after.

Also, paper lanterns over a lake are super romantic.

Disclaimer: I know that glow stick stuff is toxic or whatever, so beware if it gets in your eye and you become blind.

4: SURPRISE S'MORES AND CITY STARS

Put chaffing dish heaters or a small camping stove in a small bag with matches marshmallows, chocolate, and graham crackers. Get blankets and go outside where you can get a great view of the stars or cityscape. Get a couple small sticks and then lay out a blanket. Pull out the marshmallows, chocolate, graham crackers, and matches. Watch as their face as they put together what you are doing but are not sure how you will roast the s'mores. Pull out the chaffing dish heater or camping stove and watch them light up in smiles.

5: MINI GOLF AROUND TOWN AND IN BUILDINGS

Don't go to a mini golf course, just get a mini putting cup or make one out of a red solo cup. Take turns choosing where to place it. Outdoors, indoors, down stairs, in elevators, and so on. Get creative and then have fun.

6: SERVE SOMEONE

Get a bouquet of flowers and go to a nursing home. Ask the front desk who hasn't received visitors in a while and go make their day. Make sure you save one rose for them. Or go make bagged lunches and drop them off to the homeless.

7: PROJECTOR IN THE PARK

Get a projector and a sheet. Hang it up on a tree in a park with clamps and have your own drive-in movie.

8: CLASSIC NIGHT

Do pre-research of a classic radio broadcast (like "War of the Worlds") or movie (like *Casablanca* or *Ben Hur*) and then listen/watch it together. Get vintage candy and be a part of history together.

9: DINNER AROUND THE WORLD

Go to a library (yeah, they still have those) or a place with a globe. Have them close their eyes, spin the globe, and have them put their finger down somewhere until the globe stops. Now go research what type of food is served in that exact location, get recipes, go to the store to buy the ingredients and make yourself a trip around the world.

10: SNOW AND COCOA

Sledding, ice skating, or snow shoeing lead to snowball fights which lead to snow wrestling which leads to snow kissing which leads to hot cocoa cuddling which leads to a great next date.

11: OUTDOOR INSIGHT

A hike to a campfire, shooting targets in the boonies, making sand castles, and other outdoor activities that require a little effort and getting a little messy really lets you know a lot about someone. If you have a complainer on your hands . . . run. If they are a trooper, chase!

12: BABYSIT A FREAKING CUTE PUPPY

Find someone who has a puppy. With permission (and I *cannot* stress that enough), take it for an evening to show that puppy and your date the time of its life.

13: RESTAURANT TOUR (ESPECIALLY WITH PLACES YOU'VE NEVER BEEN)

Look online to see what restaurant has the best appetizers. Then find the one with the best main courses. And finally, find the one with the best desserts. It is most fun if they are places you've never been to before. Go and try it out. A Note: this is *not* for first dates.

14: THE QUESTION GAME

Find a game that has quick turns (I usually use Pass the Pigs or a dice game like Farkle). The winner of that round gets to ask the other person any question. Then both answer the question before the next round can begin.

15: GROUP DATE TO SINGLE FATE

A great way to have great conversation is to start the date with a bigger group date for dinner. Make sure you are both included in the group conversations. Then split off and go for dessert separately. It is a great way to minimize the initial awkward conversation and gives you plenty to discuss one-on-one.

16: BOOKSTORE STORY TIME

Go to a bookstore and read to each other your favorite children's book. It is also a great idea to read your favorite section of another book that is meaningful to you. You can really get to know a lot about someone from a simple yet revealing date like this.

ABOUT THE AUTHOR

*Z*ack Oates is an entrepreneur, hot tubber, and blogger. He has started six businesses, which have been featured in *Wired Magazine*, the *New York Times*, and the *Wall Street Journal*. He has an MBA from BYU with an emphasis in innovation and a bachelor's in advertising and marketing. He was voted one of the top 100 entrepreneurs by VSpring Capital and received first place at the largest university business plan competition in the world (over 800 teams participated). After living in Ukraine for two years serving a mission for The Church of Jesus Christ of Latter-day Saints, he started a nonprofit in 2008 called Courage to Hope, which works with victims of domestic violence in Ukraine. In addition to being a finalist and then "Love Guru" on the *Mormon Bachelor* and *Bachelorette*, he has an inspiration and dating blog called *Bowl of Oates*.

SCAN TO VISIT

bowlofoates.com